HANDBOOK

for

Los Angeles

NEWCOMER'S HANDBOOK ™

for Los Angeles

FIRST BOOKS

P.O. Box 578147
Chicago, IL 60657
(773) 276-5911

www.firstbooks.com

Author: Stacey Ravel Abarbanel
Publisher and Editor: Jeremy Solomon
Contributing Editor: Paul Herring
Cover/Interior design, production: Miles & Gale DeCoster, Art Machine, Inc.
Maps: Tom Greensfelder

ISBN 0-912301-30-9   ISSN 1086-8879

Manufactured in the United States of America.

Published by First Books, Inc., P.O. Box 578147, Chicago, IL 60657, (312) 276-5911.

  Suggestions for finding rentals in Los Angeles, what to look for in an
  apartment, leases, security deposits and rent control, mail and
  telephone, storage

WELCOME to El Pueblo de Nuestra Señora la Reina de Los Angeles (in English, the town of our lady the queen of the angels). That's the name the Spanish gave to this city when in 1781, 44 village settlers made their home in what is now downtown LA. Today, Los Angeles is a multi-ethnic, multi-cultural society as diverse as any city in the world. People from more than 140 countries live in Los Angeles County, including the largest population of Mexican, Armenian, Korean, Filipino, Salvadoran and Guatemalan communities outside their respective home nations. In general, it's safe to say that with 8.6 million people living in the county of Los Angeles, there is indeed something for everyone.

Since there are millions of Spanish speakers here and the city's roots are Hispanic too, you may find it fun and useful to pick up some Spanish phrases. That way you'll not only be able to converse with Spanish-speaking residents, but you'll also discover the meaning behind street names and civic landmarks like "La Cienega" (the swamp) and "La Brea" (the tar).

For decades, people around the world have been attracted to Los Angeles for its promises of fame and fortune, and excellent year-round weather. While only a sliver of the population is famous and wealthy, the good weather here is no myth. Average temperatures range from 58 degrees Fahrenheit in December to 76 degrees in September, yet it's not uncommon to have an 80 degree day at the beach in February, while much of the country shivers under a layer of snow.

You may notice that any time you ask a Los Angeleno how long it takes to get someplace, the answer is invariably "twenty minutes." In theory, it should take only twenty minutes to get from the Valley to the city, from the Westside to Downtown, or from the South Bay to the Westside, but unfortunately the realities of traffic (especially during rush hours) can turn a twenty minute ride into an hour-long journey.

In fact, Los Angeles' traffic and other negatives like crime and racial tensions are perhaps as famous now as are her plusses. But as someone once said of LA, "If this is Hell, why is it so popular?".

Perhaps it's because in recent decades, Los Angeles has been the first city to confront the future on all fronts: culturally, artistically, politically and socially. That confrontation can be both exciting and frightening, challenging and rewarding. It is certainly that electric feel, that sense of change, that attracts people from other cities and countries. And for those who choose to call Los Angeles "home", she welcomes you with a wealth of opportunities.

A T FIRST GLANCE, Los Angeles appears to be a sprawling metropolis, with no clear demarcations from one municipality to the next, let alone distinct neighborhoods. It takes time and patience to come to understand the seemingly subtle qualities that make Santa Monica different from Venice, or Silverlake from the Fairfax district, but after some time here, you will find that there really are neighborhoods in Los Angeles, and a large variety at that.

One way Los Angelenos are different from residents of most cities is that while they take pride and pleasure in their neighborhood, they are by no means confined to it. Certainly LA's "car culture" is partially responsible, but exploring LA's many "villages" is also easy and fun, and for newcomers especially, it's encouraged.

While cruising through the city you will no doubt encounter the "strip center" phenomenon: the fact that there appears to be a two- to three-story mini-mall on every other block. While you will hear many residents complain that these modern strip centers are eyesores on the LA streets ("Do we really need another frozen yogurt store?"), take a closer look. They may be architecturally uninspiring, but some of these strip centers have become little neighborhood commerce centers in areas that previously had none. Recently, good neighborhood restaurants have been cropping up in strip centers, alongside such useful businesses as independent Laundromats®, video stores, and yes, yogurt shops.

Los Angeles' problems of crime and violence may be notorious, but in reality they reflect our entire nation's urban woes, and are certainly no better or worse here than in other major U.S. metropolises. In fact, a recent *Money* magazine survey of FBI crime statistics ranked the fifteen most dangerous cities in the country, and Los Angeles didn't make the list. As in any city, a good dose of street smarts and common sense will help steer you away from trouble, and as safety experts are fond of reminding us, always be aware of your surroundings. Certain high-crime neighborhoods like South-Central and Watts are not recommended for outsiders or newcomers, but conversely, there are plenty of safe and affordable areas to live, work and play.

In general, you can expect the climate and air quality to be hotter and smoggier the further east you go, with the warmest temperatures and worst air pollution occurring in the summer months. For detailed information on the air quality in the areas you are considering calling home, contact the South Coast Air Quality Management District at 909-396-2000.

Due to LA's vastness, this guide does not attempt to cover every residential area, but it does cover many. Some areas are separate incorporated cities, others are simply Los Angeles neighborhoods. What follows is a list of neighborhoods and cities that newcomers should check out, complete with a description of the areas. It begins on the Westside with the beach communities, and moves more or less East, through downtown, then North with some coverage of the Valley. Other useful information such as area codes (West of La Cienega Boulevard is 310; East of La Cienega Boulevard is 213; the Valley is 818), zip codes, nearby post offices, district police stations, neighborhood hospitals, and public libraries will follow each neighborhood description. The neighborhood boundaries are in some cases approximations, since areas that are not distinct cities tend to blend into one another.

The following neighborhoods are profiled:

Malibu

Topanga Canyon

Santa Monica

Venice

Marina del Rey

Playa del Rey

Manhattan Beach

Inglewood

Mar Vista and Palms

Culver City

West Los Angeles

Brentwood

Westwood

Beverly Hills

West Hollywood

Fairfax District

Hollywood

Los Feliz/Silverlake/Echo Park

Leimert Park

Downtown

Pasadena

San Fernando Valley

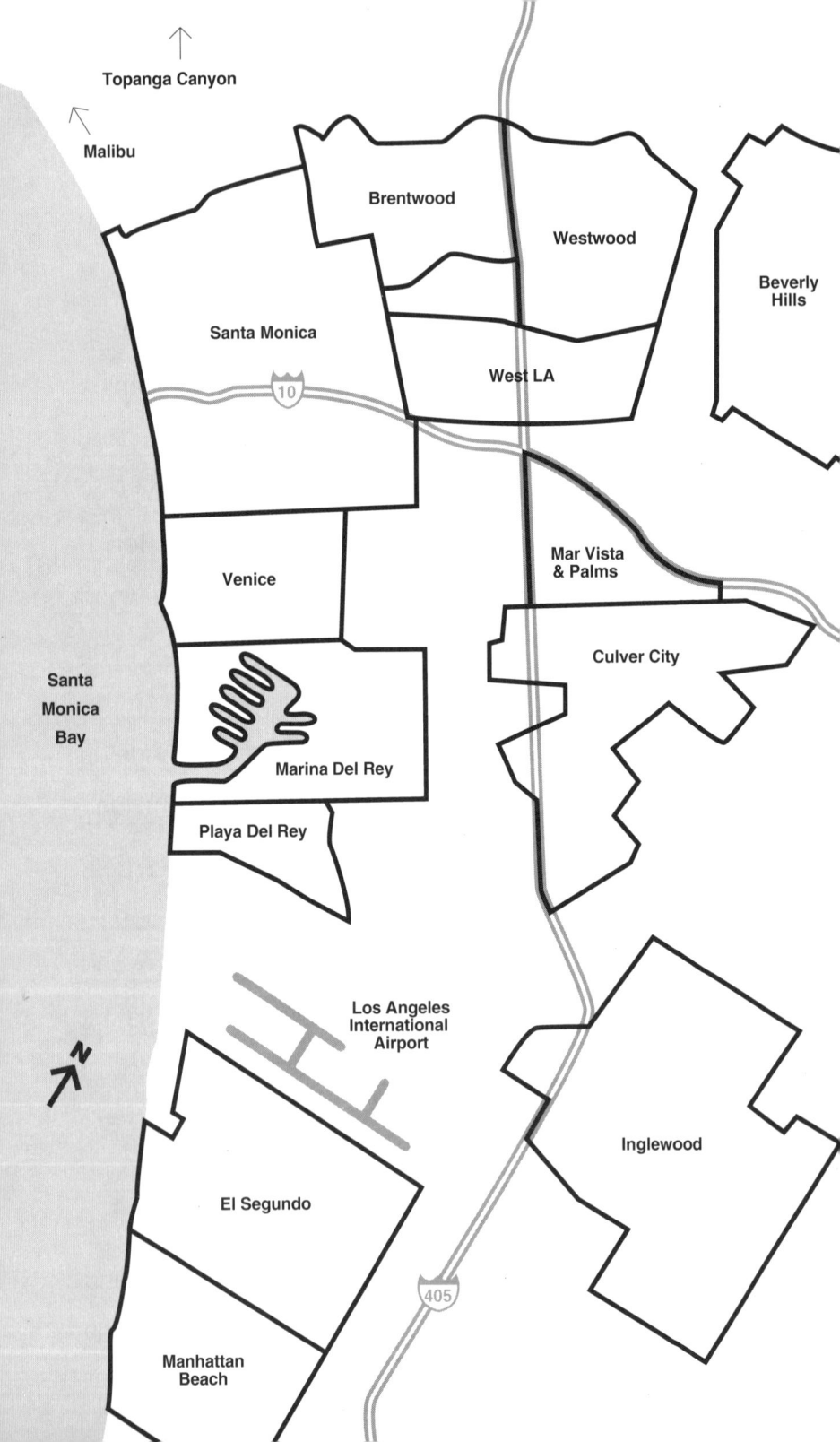

Malibu

Boundaries: North: Mulholland Highway; **East:** Tuna Canyon Road, Saddle Creek Road; **South:** Santa Monica Bay; **West:** Mulholland Highway

"Malibu—it's a state of mind." This message seen on license plate holders across Los Angeles may leave you scratching your head and wondering what it all means...until you get to Malibu. Because once you travel twenty miles northwest of Santa Monica on the Pacific Coast Highway (PCH, to those in the know) and make it to Malibu, you may find that it is not so much a place as a peaceful vibe, often absent in other parts of the region.

In fact, upon arrival Malibu is not so impressive. You'll find fast-food stands, small shopping centers, and surf shops, sprinkled with a few fancy restaurants like Wolfgang Puck's star hangout, Granita. The pretty Malibu Pier offers fishing and food. Most non-residents come to Malibu for the beaches, which are some of the loveliest and cleanest (both sand and ocean water) in the Los Angeles area. Zuma Beach is the most crowded, nearby Point Dume is a bit less populated, and Leo Carillo, a 1,600-acre beach the furthest northwest, features three campgrounds. Surfrider Beach is still popular with surfers, as it was in the 50's and 60's when Annette Funicello and Frankie Avalon frolicked here in their *Beach Blanket Bingo* movies.

As for residents, Malibu is the home, or second home (or third, or fourth), to the rich and famous who like its scenery and privacy. The most well-known spot for celebrities to live is the Malibu Beach Colony, a gated community right on the sand. Note that while the streets and homes in the Colony are not reachable to outsiders, the ocean is. The tidelands in California, defined as the area below the mean high tide, are considered public land. Hence, you can park along the road before or after the Colony property (or, for that matter, almost any other private beach area in the state), and walk along the wet, packed sand for a look at these beach-side villas. A few private beach communities have guards that will chase you off the dry, sandy part of the beach, but stick to the hard, wet sand along the tide and you should be okay.

Aside from famous folks, Malibu has a fair share of successful professionals, surfer dudes and dudettes, and just plain beach lovers living in its midst. Most are drawn to the area because living here offers proximity to Los Angeles, without all the city-life hustle-bustle. As you might imagine, rents and house prices in Malibu are most expensive at the coast, and then decrease as you move inland, into the canyons. While the area is mostly owner-occupied, there are some apartments, condominiums, and homes for rent.

Because much of Malibu is hilly, dry canyon country, brush fires are a problem here almost every summer. Then in the winter, since some of the vegetation has been burned away, winter rains can cause land slides, which then cause flooding. Through it all, most residents say the privacy and beauty of Malibu make it worthwhile.

Area Code: 310.

Zip Codes: 90265, 90264.

Post Offices: Main Post Office, 23838 West Pacific Coast Highway, 456-2018; La Costa Station, 21229 West Pacific Coast Highway, 456-8260; Point Dume Station, 29160 West Heathercliff Road, 457-3017.

Police Department: Malibu is served by the Los Angeles County Sheriff's Department, 27050 Agoura Road, Agoura, 818-878-1808.

Emergency Hospitals: Malibu Medical Clinic, 23656 Pacific Coast Highway, 456-7551; Santa Monica UCLA Medical Center, 1250 16th Street, 319-4000.

Library: Malibu Library, 23519 Civic Center Way, 456-6438.

Topanga Canyon

Boundaries: North: Mulholland Drive; **East:** Topanga State Park; **South:** Santa Monica Bay; **West:** Las Flores Canyon

Curvy mountain roads, tangled trees and vines, an occasional hippie-type hitchhiking alongside the canyon passage way—are we in LA? Nestled in the Santa Monica Mountains between Santa Monica and Malibu, Topanga Canyon hardly seems like a part of a major metropolis. Its roots are still firmly planted in the hippie, artist, and other alternative communities that have populated this unincorporated part of Los Angeles County for decades.

It's easy to see why people choose to live in Topanga Canyon. For starters, there is the beautiful, natural setting, complete with vistas (in some spots) of the Pacific Ocean. Another bonus is the relatively low cost of housing in the area. Residences run the gamut from mountain cabins to newer, high-end houses, and rents and home prices are much cheaper than in nearby, chic Malibu. In recent years city residents have discovered that Topanga is more than just a good place to take a day hike, hence today your next-door neighbor here is as likely to be a Downtown lawyer as a stained-glass artist.

However, people used to the convenience of home-delivered Chinese food or 2 a.m. grocery shopping should think twice about living in Topanga Canyon. Although only a few miles down Pacific Coast Highway from Pacific Palisades, Topanga feels remote. At the crest of Topanga Canyon Road there is a neighborhood grocery market, video store, gas station, and a few other businesses, but for the most part, once you've driven up the hill towards home, you've probably left the day's errands behind. And that's just the way Topanga Canyonites like it. Hikers frequent Topanga Canyon, especially along the beautiful, hilly trails at Topanga State Park. Another neat spot in the Canyon is the Will Geer Theatricum Botanicum, a rustic outdoor theater now headed by actor Will Geer's daughter Ellen, where in the summer you can have a picnic, then sit under the stars on comfy throw pillows and see Shakespeare and other plays and musical productions.

Finally, it's worth noting that if big rains hit during the winter, Topanga Canyon Boulevard often washes out for a day or so, especially along the creek beds.

Area Code: 310.

Zip Code: 90290.

Post Office: 101 South Topanga Canyon Boulevard, 455-1134.

Police Department: Topanga Canyon is served by the Los Angeles County Sheriff's Department, 27050 Agoura Road, Agoura, 27050, 818-878-1808.

Emergency Hospitals: Santa Monica UCLA Medical Center, 1250 16th Street, Santa Monica, 319-4000; St. John's Hospital & Health Center, 1328 22nd Street, Santa Monica, 829-5511.

Libraries: Malibu Library, 23519 Civic Center Way, Malibu, 456-6438; Palisades, 861 Alma Real Drive, Pacific Palisades, 459-2754.

Santa Monica

Boundaries: North: San Vicente Boulevard; **East:** Centinela Avenue; **South:** Dewey Street; **West:** Santa Monica Bay, Pacific Ocean

Nicknamed "Santa Moscow" for its liberal city politics, Santa Monica is a highly coveted neighborhood, both for its seaside location and rent-controlled apartments. Residents like to brag that the air is cleaner and the weather cooler here than anywhere else in LA, and it's probably true. While summer temperatures in Los Angeles can hover in the 80's and 90's, it's not uncommon for Santa Monica to sport temperatures that are 15 degrees cooler than Downtown or the Valley. In the past few years, tourists and trendsetters have "found" Santa Monica, and three main areas in this small city (it measures only 8.3 square miles) come to life each day with shops, art galleries, restaurants and movie theaters.

The area around Main Street is probably the hippest and beachiest. Main Street itself houses art galleries, restaurants, bars, and shops, and the coffee houses overflow with cool singles or young families with strollers in tow. To the West of Main Street are several walking lanes lined with some nice and some run-down beach cottages, but regardless, prices are high due to the proximity to the ocean. The hilly neighborhood just East of Main Street consists of apartments and condominiums, with a few funky old houses mixed in.

Downtown Santa Monica is centered around a lively outdoor mall called the Third Street Promenade, with shops, restaurants, and a multitude of movie theaters that attract huge crowds (and enterprising street performers) on the weekends. The Promenade is also a Mecca for book lovers, with the largest concentration of corporate superstores, fine used book stores, and specialized independent book shops anywhere in the Los Angeles area.

Like much of Los Angeles, the neighborhoods in Santa Monica tend to get more high-end as you move North, and true to form, the area North of upscale shopping street Montana Avenue features some of LA's most beautiful (and priciest) homes. Luckily for those less financially-endowed, the area South of Montana Avenue sports mostly apartments and condominiums, while still boasting access to the area's cafes, coffeehouses, and shops.

If all this sounds too good to be true, consider the following: It is *very difficult* to find an apartment in Santa Monica. Historically, rent control has kept the prices low and created an environment where apartments are "passed down" like family heirlooms, and rarely does a good rent-controlled unit come on the open market. Also, some buildings are run-down, since landlords say the low rents don't allow them enough income to make improvements. However, as of January 1, 1996, a new state law altered Santa Monica's strict rent control. Once an apartment becomes voluntarily vacated, landlords can now raise rents 15%. This should garner more money for improvements to the units, but it will also eventually eliminate "steals" for newcomers to the city.

The best way to find a place is to ask around, and even drive or walk through the areas you are interested in to see if there are any vacancies. Or, you may have luck finding units through the classified advertisements in the local paper, the *Santa Monica Outlook.*

Finally, some people may be uncomfortable living in what local radio personality Harry Shearer refers to as "The Home of the Homeless". Of late the city has been successful in cleaning up local parks like Lincoln and Palisades, which were overrun by homeless people and therefore under-utilized by other residents. However, the favorable weather and relatively tolerant government have made Santa Monica a haven for homeless people, who tend to congregate around downtown, the civic center, and in some parks.

Area Code: 310.

Zip Codes: 90401—90406.

Post Offices: Main Post Office, 1248 5th Street, 576-2626;

Ocean Park Station, 2720 Neilson Way, 576-2620: Will Rogers Station, 1217 Wilshire Boulevard, 576-2616.

Police Department: Santa Monica is served by its own municipal police force. Headquarters: 1685 Main Street, 395-9931.

Emergency Hospitals: Santa Monica UCLA Medical Center, 1250 16th Street, 319-4000; St. John's Hospital & Health Center, 1328 22nd Street, 829-5511.

Libraries: Main Library, 1343 6th Street, 458-8600; Fairview Branch, 2101 Ocean Park Boulevard, 450-0443; Montana Avenue Branch, 1704 Montana Avenue, 829-7081; Ocean Park Branch, 2601 Main Street, 392-3804.

Transportation: Big Blue Bus, 1660 7th Street, 451-5444.

Venice

Boundaries: North: Dewey Street; **East:** Walgrove Avenue; **South:** Washington Street; **West:** Santa Monica Bay, Pacific Ocean

The funkiest of Los Angeles' beach communities, Venice is an eclectic mix of artists, surfers, bodybuilders, and sightseers. It was founded in 1900 by Abbot Kinney, whose dream was to foster a cultural renaissance in America by recreating an Italian "Venice" here. Some of the area's original Venetian-style architecture still stands near the boardwalk, as do a few of the canals. Despite these Venetian touches, it is doubtful that Abbot Kinney had any idea just what kind of culture Venice would become known for.

Yes, men and women in skimpy bathing suits *do* rollerblade™ down the streets here. And yes, burly muscle men and women *do* perform their workouts and flex for tourists at Muscle Beach. But Venice is also home to a strong and thriving artists' community, composed of first-rate studios, galleries, and artists' residences. The heart of the area is Ocean Front Walk (known as the boardwalk), a beach front collection of shops, outdoor cafes, street performers, jewelry and sunglasses stands, and the liveliest place in town to get your palm read, hair braided, or back massaged. Housing runs the gamut from beach cottages to reasonably priced apartments to ocean-front villas. Prices vary greatly, but generally the closer you are to the ocean, the more you pay.

East of the boardwalk is Abbot Kinney Boulevard. While this street hasn't caught on like its Santa Monica neighbor Main Street (and some think that's just fine), it features a sparse but interesting mix of art galleries, antique stores, restaurants, and shops. The surrounding homes and apartments are somewhat run down, but there are a few old gems and some contemporary buildings mixed in amongst the rest. Each Spring the Venice Family Clinic hosts a fund-raiser, the Venice ArtWalk, when artists open their studios and homes for a large walking tour of the area. The canal neighborhood offers one of LA's most charming living situations. The houses along the canals vary from ramshackle cottages to newly built mini-mansions, but the feel of the area is still charming. Ducks swim along the canals, and many residents have their own row boats for tooling through the area. Even if you don't care to live here, it's certainly worth a stroll or drive (take Dell Avenue north from Washington Boulevard).

While Venice's proximity to the beach and boardwalk and general outdoor lifestyle are definite plusses, beware that crime here is higher than average, as rough neighborhoods are adjacent to the area.

Area Code: 310.

Zip Code: 90291.

Post Office: Main Post Office, 1601 Main Street, 396-3191.

Police District: Pacific Division, 12312 Culver Boulevard, 202-4502.

Emergency Hospital: Daniel Freeman Marina Hospital, 4650 Lincoln Boulevard, 823-8911.

Library: Venice Branch, 501 South Venice Boulevard, 310-821-1769.

Marina del Rey

Boundaries: North: Washington Street; **East:** Centinela Boulevard; **South:** Bollona Creek; **West:** Santa Monica Bay, Pacific Ocean

Situated around a pleasure harbor, Marina del Rey has a reputation as a singles area. Fitness-minded and largely professionals, the residents enjoy the Marina's waterfront locale and proximity to boating, sailing, wind surfing, water-skiing, tennis, and jogging and bicycling paths. The population of Marina del Rey is quite homogenous, with approximately 70% aged 25-54 and approximately 90% white.

The area known as the Marina Peninsula is a strip of land between the ocean and the boat harbor, and is composed of streets and walkways that run perpendicular to the beach. Locals use the alphabetical, nautical street names, "Anchorage" down to "Yawl", to refer not only to the streets themselves but to the beaches they abut, i.e. "Let's meet at 'Driftwood' at

11:30." The Marina Peninsula sports both large, upscale mini-mansions and more traditional beach cottages and apartments.

There is an abundance of modern apartments throughout the rest of Marina del Rey, many featuring gyms, swimming pools and tennis courts. Prices can be high for all these amenities and the good location, so many young professionals fresh out of college team up here as house mates.

In December the area where the boats are moored lights up with the Marina del Rey Christmas Boat Parade. Boat owners cover their decks with hundreds of twinkly lights, then promenade along the waterways in the Marina. This spectacle is free of charge, and beautiful, to boot.

Area Code: 310.

Zip Code: 90292.

Post Office: Marina del Rey Branch, 4736 Admiralty Way, 306-1233.

Police District: Pacific Division, 12312 Culver Boulevard, 202-4502.

Emergency Hospital: Daniel Freeman Marina Hospital, 4650 Lincoln Boulevard, 823-8911.

Library: Marina del Rey Branch, 4533 Admiralty Way, 821-3415.

Playa del Rey

Boundaries: North: Bollona Creek; **East:** Lincoln Boulevard, **South:** Manchester Avenue; **West:** Pacific Ocean

Residents say Playa del Rey (Spanish for King's Beach) is their little private hideaway. Isolated from the rest of Los Angeles by wetlands and featuring a shack-style downtown strip of Mom and Pop restaurants and shops, Playa del Rey has the feel of a small California beach town. Since there are no public parking lots and street parking is limited, the beaches in Playa are relatively uncrowded, even during the hot summer months. For years there has been talk of developing the wetlands, once owned by Howard Hughes, with an office/residential park or movie production facilities, and recently the city council voted to allow such development. So far the wetlands remain relatively untouched, a vacant but effective barrier from the rest of the city. However, with the recent announcement of Dreamworks' planned move to Playa Vista, change may come fast.

Lower Playa del Rey consists of the few streets right along the beach, and features mostly modern townhouses, condominiums and apartments. Up on Manchester Avenue is Upper Playa del Rey, and with the exception of some housing that offers magnificent views, this residential area is considered a bit less desirable than the spots right down by the water. On the other hand, if you're looking to rent or buy a house, they are found only in this upper area.

Playa del Rey is just north of Los Angeles International Airport (known as LAX), and that fact can be a plus or a minus, depending on your needs. Frequent travelers will appreciate the light commute to the airport, but the noise of the incoming and outgoing planes, especially in Upper Playa del Rey, can be a nuisance.

Prospective residents might also like to know that Playa del Rey is the sight of the Hyperion Treatment Plant, a sewage treatment facility at 12000 Vista del Mar. The Department of Public Works assures that state-of-the-art technology is used to both monitor the environmental impact of the plant and to maintain safe standards. If you would like more information on the environmental monitoring of the plant, contact the public relations department at 310-648-5217.

Area Code: 310.

Zip Code: 90293.

Post Office: Playa del Rey Branch, 215 Culver Boulevard, 823-6006.

Police District: Pacific Division, 12312 Culver Boulevard, 202-4502.

Emergency Hospital: Daniel Freeman Marina Hospital, 4650 Lincoln Boulevard, 823-8911.

Library: Marina del Rey Branch, 4533 Admiralty Way, 821-3415.

El Segundo

Boundaries: North: Imperial Highway; **East:** Aviation Boulevard; **South:** Rosecrans Boulevard; **West:** Vista del Mar Boulevard

Located directly south of Los Angeles International Airport and fourteen miles southwest of Downtown LA, the city of El Segundo is so named because in 1911, Standard Oil Company selected it as the site of its second oil refinery—hence the name El Segundo, which is Spanish for "the second." In fact, a 1920's newspaper advertisement described the town as "the Standard Oil payroll city." The 1,000-acre refinery is still a major part of El Segundo, encompassing the southwestern quadrant of the city. The rest of the city is 80% zoned for commercial/industrial use, and 20% is composed of the tranquil residential enclave west of Sepulveda.

In addition to the oil refinery, El Segundo is also a hub for the aviation and defense industries. By the late 1980's, thousands of people worked here, due to a large number of defense contracts handled by companies like Hughes, Rockwell, Northrop, TRW, and Aerospace Corporation. Defense contracts waned in the early 90's and the number of workers was drastically reduced, but recently contracts appear to be on the rise.

A plus for residents and workers alike is the fact that El Segundo boasts one of the lowest crime rates in Los Angeles County, accomplished in part by having more police per capita than most small cities and the highest ratio in the region. Recently, the Metropolitan Transit Authority opened the Green Line in El Segundo, providing rail line service twenty miles east to Norwalk.

You can expect most of the housing here to be modern and rather nondescript. The 15,000 residents love the area's small-town atmosphere, but due to its close proximity to the airport (LAX), overhead noise can be a problem. However, if your job requires a lot of flying, that nearness to the airport can be a plus. Also, intermittent fumes from the Hyperion sewage treatment plant (see section on **Playa del Rey**) have given the area the nickname "El Stinko."

According to the Chamber of Commerce, rentals for apartments and duplexes range from $550 to $1,440 per month, and rentals for houses range from $1,000 to $1,500 per month. The weekly *El Segundo Herald* includes a listing of rentals in its classified advertisements.

Area Code: 310.

Zip Code: 90245.

Post Office: 200 Main Street, 322-1476.

Police Department: El Segundo is served by its own municipal police force. Headquarters: 348 Main Street, 322-9114.

Emergency Hospitals: Centinela Medical Center, 455 Main Street, 322-1611; Daniel Freeman LAX Medical Clinic, 815 North Sepulveda Boulevard, 322-5393.

Library: El Segundo Library, 111 West Mariposa Avenue, 322-4121.

Manhattan Beach

Boundaries: North: Rosecrans Avenue; **East:** Aviation Boulevard; **South:** Artesia Boulevard; **West:** Pacific Ocean

Ever wonder what happened to Susie Sorority and Frank Fraternity after graduation? They moved to Manhattan Beach. It may be a bit more of a commute to work, but the young residents here (the average age is 32)

think the beautiful beaches and lively shops, restaurants and bars are worth the drive.

Beach life here centers around The Strand, a cement promenade popular with skaters, joggers, and walkers, and the South Bay Bicycle Trail that also runs along the beach. The sand itself is popular with sunbathers and volleyball players, who can choose their game site from more than one hundred courts.

A short walk from the city's white, sandy beach is the vibrant, charming shopping district centered around Manhattan Avenue and Manhattan Beach Boulevard. The area is densely packed with cafes, bars, bookstores and clothing shops, and weekend nights resemble those in a college town, with scores of young adults walking the streets and taking in the local bar and restaurant scene.

Housing options near the ocean include quaint beach cottages and multi-unit apartment buildings. Since Manhattan Beach is on a slight hill, many units boast ocean views, and rents for these units are higher. The area east of Ardmore Avenue is family-oriented, with mostly single family houses. It is important to note that although Manhattan Beach is located only about 20 miles southwest of downtown Los Angeles, the weekday commute to downtown can be as long as 45 minutes to over an hour, each way. If your job requires a lot of flying, though, Manhattan Beach is conveniently near the airport (LAX).

Area Code: 310.

Zip Code: 90266.

Post Offices: Main Post Office, 1007 N. Sepulveda Boulevard, 647-1715; Substation, 425 15th Street, 545-1695.

Police Department: Manhattan Beach is served by its own municipal police force. Headquarters: 420 15th Street, 545-8867.

Emergency Hospital: Medical Center of Manhattan Beach, 2809 North Sepulveda Boulevard, 546-4606.

Libraries: Main Library, 1320 Highland Avenue, 545-8595; Manhattan Heights, 1560 Manhattan Beach Boulevard, 379-8401.

Inglewood

Boundaries: North: 64th Street; **East:** Van Ness Avenue; **South:** Imperial Highway; **West:** 405 Freeway

Sports fans know Inglewood as the home of The Great Western Forum, site of the Los Angeles Lakers' home basketball games and The Kings' home ice hockey games. It is also the site of Hollywood Park horse race track. Downtown Inglewood is centered around Market Street and Manchester Avenue, and is a true neighborhood shopping district offering such useful amenities as grocery stores, pharmacies, and hair salons. According to 1990 Census figures, approximately 52% of Inglewood's population is African-American, and an additional 39% is Hispanic. Much of the housing in this city consists of single-family homes, but there are also a good number of multi-unit apartment buildings. Rental prices in Inglewood are less expensive than in many of the areas north and west of the city. According to the Chamber of Commerce, rentals for one and two bedroom apartments range from $500 to $1,000 per month, and rentals for two and three bedroom houses range from $600 to $1,000 per month.

Area Code: 310.

Zip Codes: 90301—90305.

Post Offices: Main Post Office, 300 East Hillcrest, 674-1625; Crenshaw Imperial Station, 2672 West Imperial Highway, 755-5864; Lennox Branch, 4443 Lennox Boulevard, 674-7834; Morningside Park Station, 3212 West 85th Street, 778-3739; North Station, 811 North La Brea Avenue, 674-6638.

Police Department: Inglewood is served by its own municipal police force. Headquarters: 1 Manchester Boulevard, 412-5210.

Emergency Hospitals: Daniel Freeman Memorial Hospital, 333 North Prairie Avenue, 674-7050; Centinela Hospital, 555 E. Hardy Street, 673-4660.

Libraries: Main Library, 101 West Manchester Boulevard, 412-5380; Crenshaw Imperial Branch, 11141 Crenshaw Boulevard, 412-5403; Morningside Park Branch, 3202 West 85th Street, 412-5400.

Mar Vista and Palms

Boundaries: North: 10 Freeway; **East:** Motor Avenue; **South:** Venice Boulevard; **West:** 405 Freeway

Just northwest of Culver City are two neighborhoods that lie within the boundaries of the city of Los Angeles: Mar Vista, and a bit further east, Palms. There is a small commercial center in Palms of neighborhood restaurants and a few stores along Motor Avenue between Venice and National Boulevards, but for the most part, what attracts people to Mar Vista and Palms is the plentiful number of reasonably priced apartment and home rentals in this easy-to-access Westside location. They are also popular areas for first-time home buyers, since housing prices are lower that most other Westside locales. Of the two neighborhoods, Mar Vista is more geared toward family living. It has more single family homes and fewer apartment buildings than Palms, and the affordable home prices are attractive to young families. A few streets atop the hill in Mar Vista boast ocean and city views. As evidence of the population in this area, Mar Vista Park at Mc Laughlin and Palms is usually filled with families (or kids with nannies) using the facilities, and the recreation department there caters to children with summer camps, gym classes, and toddler programs.

The southernmost boundary for both Palms and Mar Vista, Venice Boulevard, is a commercial strip seemingly overflowing with business where you can find everything from ethnic food to discount futons. A short drive or walk north on Motor Avenue just under the 10 Freeway leads to lovely Cheviot Hills, a hilly (as the name implies) residential neighborhood of mostly vintage Southern California homes. Continuing north on Motor Avenue will lead to Cheviot Hills Park, a large park offering 14 lit tennis courts, archery, swimming, basketball courts, baseball diamonds, and Rancho Park, reputed to be one of the busiest public golf courses in the country. Motor Avenue runs north into the Twentieth Century Fox studio lot, and although it's closed to the public, you can spot the old movie set street from "Hello, Dolly" as you drive by.

Area Code: 310.

Zip Code: 90034.

Post Offices: Mar Vista Station, 3865 Grand View Boulevard, 390-3491; Palms Station, 3751 Motor Avenue, 839-1181.

Police District: Pacific Division, 12312 Culver Boulevard, 202-4502.

Emergency Hospital: Brotman Medical Center, 3828 Delmas Terrace, 836-7000.

Libraries: Mar Vista Branch, 12006 Venice Boulevard, 390-3454; Palms-Rancho Park Branch, 2920 Overland Avenue, 838-2157.

Culver City

Boundaries: North: Venice Boulevard; **East:** Jefferson Boulevard; **South:** Slauson Avenue **West:** 405 Freeway

Culver City is the original *and* current home to several major movie studios, including the landmark site of Metro Goldwyn Mayer, now the home of Sony Studios. Such movie classics as "Citizen Kane", "King Kong", "ET" and the scene of Atlanta burning in "Gone With the Wind" were all filmed on the lots of Culver City movie studios.

Though only five square miles and bordered on all sides by parts of LA, Culver City is its own municipal entity. As a workplace hub, the industrial area known as the Hayden Tract, located between National Boulevard and Higuera Street and north of Bollona Creek, is undergoing a unique renaissance. Most of these industrial buildings were constructed in the 1940's, and while the space was formerly occupied by traditional manufacturing and assembly operations, those businesses are being replaced by design and art studios, high-tech marketing firms, and architecture offices. In the past few years, two unique buildings designed by award-winning architect Eric Owen Moss, "The Box" on National Boulevard and another project on Hayden Avenue, have also focused attention on this area for their eye-catching appearance.

A lot of the hustle-bustle at cafes and stores along Washington Boulevard is due to the daytime traffic generated by local businesses, but the 38,000 residents enjoy a much less hurried pace in the evenings, once everyone else has gone home. In addition, the downtown area has recently undergone major improvements, with new construction and streetscaping of shopping areas, such as Bagley Avenue.

Although much of Culver City is zoned for commercial, industrial and light industrial business, there are also pockets of single-family homes and apartment buildings. According to the Chamber of Commerce, rentals for one-to-three bedroom apartments and duplexes range from $700 to $1,400 monthly, and rentals for one-to-three bedroom houses range from $900 to $1,800 per month. First-time home buyers might want to consider Culver City, which offers lower home and condominium prices than much of the Westside and is close to both the Santa Monica (10) and the San Diego (405) Freeways.

Area Code: 310.

Zip Codes: 90230, 90232.

Post Offices: Main Post Office, 1111 Jefferson Boulevard, 391-6374; Fox Hills Station, 6083 Bristol Parkway, 645-0173; Gateway Station, 9942 Culver Boulevard, 204-1051.

Police Department: Culver City is served by its own municipal police force. Headquarters: 4040 Duquesne Avenue, 837-1221.

Emergency Hospitals: Brotman Medical Center, 3828 Delmas Terrace, 836-7000; Washington Medical Center, 12101 West Washington Boulevard, 391-0601.

Library: Culver City Library, 4975 Overland Avenue, 559-1676.

Transportation: Culver City Municipal Bus Lines, 9815 Jefferson Boulevard, 202-5731.

West Los Angeles

Boundaries: North: Santa Monica Boulevard; **East:** Beverly Glen Boulevard; **South:** Pico Boulevard; **West:** Centinela Avenue

The area known as West LA tends to be less expensive than nearby Westwood and Brentwood, and still centrally located on the Westside. Though not as popular as some other Westside neighborhoods, West Los Angeles offers more affordable housing, as well as convenient access to both the Santa Monica (10) and the San Diego (405) Freeways. Don't expect much in the way of architectural charm, but this area is a good choice for people on a budget who want to live on the Westside.

Aficionados of Japanese food and culture should check out Sawtelle Boulevard north of Olympic Boulevard. A mini-Japan Town has developed here, with a good number of Japanese restaurants and Japanese-owned nurseries. Also worth a visit is the funky Art Deco movie house called the Nuart (on Santa Monica Boulevard just West of the 405 Freeway), which features foreign and other non-mainstream films, plus a weekly Saturday midnight showing of "The Rocky Horror Picture Show."

If you like to shop, you should know that West LA is also the locale of two of the Westside's most popular malls, the indoor Westside Pavilion and the outdoor Century City Shopping Mall.

Area Code: 310.

Zip Code: 90025.

Post Office: West Los Angeles Branch, 11420 Santa Monica Boulevard, 477-1539.

Police District: West Los Angeles Division, 1663 Butler Avenue, 575-8401.

Emergency Hospital: UCLA Medical Center, 10833 Le Conte Avenue, 825-9111.

Library: West Los Angeles Regional Branch, 11360 Santa Monica Boulevard, 575-8323.

Brentwood

Boundaries: North: Sunset Boulevard; **East:** 405 Freeway; **South:** Wilshire Boulevard; **West:** Centinela Avenue

Nowadays, it's impossible to mention Brentwood without immediately thinking of the O.J. Simpson murder trial. True, Brentwood is where the murders took place, and it is also the site of O.J. Simpson's Rockingham Avenue mansion. Thankfully, the neighborhood has more to recommend it.

Brentwood's central position on the Westside and numerous apartment buildings make it a natural for young professionals. Although it doesn't have as much character as some other Los Angeles locales, many newcomers choose Brentwood for its safe location, close-by shopping, abundant apartments, and moderately upscale atmosphere.

While the northwestern-most part of Brentwood is an affluent residential area of palatial homes on shady streets, the regions south and east of that high-end area are populated with modern-style apartment and condominium buildings. Most buildings feature off-street parking either included in the rent or for a small additional monthly fee.

The area near Brentwood Village, the quaint shopping area where Barrington Avenue meets Sunset Boulevard, offers the rare added attraction of being within walking distance of the neighborhood's cafes, bakeries, hair salons, post office, and park. Busy San Vicente Boulevard runs through the middle of Brentwood, and features upscale dining and shopping opportunities. The street has a wide park strip running all the way to the coastline in Santa Monica, making it a popular jogging and walking spot.

Sometime in 1996, the Brentwood Hills will be the home of the new J. Paul Getty Center. It's hard to miss this vast group of structures being built on a hill off the 405 Freeway. When completed, the Center will house the Getty Museum and its entire art collection save the antiquities, as well as the Getty Trust, Conservation Institute, Center for the History of the Arts and Humanities, Art History Information Program, and Center for Education in the Arts. Designed by noted architect Richard Meier, the Center is a much ballyhooed addition to Brentwood and the Los Angeles art community.

Area Code: 310.

Zip Code: 90049.

Post Office: Barrington Station, 200 S. Barrington Avenue, 476-3065.

Police District: West Los Angeles Division, 1663 Butler Avenue, 575-8401.

Emergency Hospital: UCLA Medical Center, 10833 Le Conte Avenue, 825-9111.

Library: Brentwood Branch, 11820 San Vicente Boulevard, 575-8016.

Westwood

Boundaries: North: Sunset Boulevard; **East:** Beverly Glen Boulevard; **South:** Santa Monica Boulevard; **West:** 405 Freeway

South of the tony hills of Bel Air lies Westwood, most famous for being the home of the University of California at Los Angeles (UCLA). The area around the campus is filled with fraternities, sororities, and student-inhabited apartment buildings, but non-students also enjoy the proximity to Westwood Village's many shops, restaurants, and famous movie theaters, as well as the sporting and cultural events on campus.

During the 1980's Westwood Village was *the place* for young people to hang out on the weekends. At night the crowds often got so big that police were forced to close most of the Village streets to automobiles, and allow only foot traffic.

Sadly, during the late 80's and early 90's, the congestion and a high concentration of youths in the area got out of hand, and on a few occasions screenings of violent and/or race-related movies touched off riots and looting. Additionally, Westwood Village became the too-frequent site of muggings and other crimes. Westwood Village's popularity as a destination declined, and many once-thriving businesses were forced to close.

Lately however, local merchants have had success encouraging people to return to Westwood Village, which still offers a large variety of shopping, dining and entertainment options. In fact, some Westsiders prefer to take in dinner and movie in Westwood, since it is far less crowded than Santa Monica's very popular Third Street Promenade.

Apartment rentals in Westwood can be expensive, because the large student population continually has a need for housing close to campus. The part of Westwood that is south of Wilshire Boulevard can be slightly cheaper for rentals, due to its distance from the UCLA campus. On the other end of the spectrum, the northern portion of Westwood east of the campus is a beautiful residential neighborhood of stately single-family homes.

Area Code: 310.

Zip Code: 90024

Post Office: Village Station, 11000 Wilshire Boulevard, 235-7771.

Police District: West Los Angeles Division, 1663 Butler Avenue, 575-8401.

Emergency Hospital: UCLA Medical Center, 10833 Le Conte Avenue, 825-9111.

Library: West Los Angeles Regional Branch, 11360 Santa Monica Boulevard, 575-8323.

Beverly Hills

Boundaries: North: Hills above Sunset Boulevard; **East:** Doheny Drive; **South:** Whitworth Drive; **West:** Whittier Drive

The above boundaries are rough outlines of Beverly Hills, so be cautioned: residents are *very particular* about what constitutes a Beverly Hills address. There's even something called "Beverly Hills PO," which refers to a few remote hill areas that may not look like Beverly Hills on the map, but carry a Beverly Hills post office address and therefore entitle the people who live there to Beverly Hills' civic amenities. One reason that locals are concerned about who's in and who's not is that as its own city, and a well-funded one at that, Beverly Hills municipal services (police, fire, public education, etc.) are considered superior to most of the rest of the Los Angeles area.

Due to the community's worldwide reputation as the home of the rich and famous, you might automatically discount the idea of living in "BH". And, while the homes here are beyond the reach of the average person, there are some affordably priced and beautiful, classic apartments in the area known as "below the tracks."

There really were train tracks that ran through Beverly Hills along Santa Monica Boulevard, and though now removed, the site serves to mark the "high rent" from the "low rent" district of the city. Basically, downtown Beverly Hills (including the famous Rodeo Drive) starts south of Santa Monica Boulevard and continues south to Wilshire Boulevard. Along Wilshire Boulevard are high-rise office buildings, large upscale department stores (Neiman-Marcus, Saks Fifth Avenue and Barney's), and the stately Regent Beverly Wilshire Hotel.

South of Wilshire Boulevard is the area where relatively reasonable apartments and flats are located. Most of these buildings feature the beautiful original, Spanish-style architecture, and many offer hardwood floors, molded ceilings, and stained or leaded glass windows. Harder to find but worth hunting for are the gatehouses and apartments over garages that are part of many of the Beverly Hills homes in "the flats," the often palm tree-lined residential streets between Sunset and Santa Monica Boulevards, and to a lesser extent in the hills above Sunset Boulevard. For assistance locating housing in BH, you might want to

check out the classified ads in the local newspaper, the *Beverly Hills Courier.*

Area Code: 310.

Zip Codes: 90210—90212.

Post Offices: Main Post Office, 325 North Maple Drive, 247-3400; Beverly Station, 312 S. Beverly Drive, 247-3458; Crescent Station, 469 N. Crescent Drive, 247-3451; Eastgate Station, 8383 Wilshire Boulevard, 247-3461.

Police Department: Beverly Hills is served by its own municipal police force. Headquarters: 464 North Rexford Drive, 550-4800.

Emergency Hospital: Cedars-Sinai Medical Center, 8700 Beverly Boulevard, 855-5000.

Library: 444 North Rexford Drive, 288-2220.

West Hollywood

Boundaries: North: Sunset Boulevard (to the West), Fountain Avenue (to the East); **East:** La Brea Avenue; **South:** Beverly Boulevard (to the West), Willoughby Avenue (to the East); **West:** Doheny Drive

West Hollywood made headlines in 1984 when the city incorporated with America's first openly gay mayor, Valerie Terrigno. Though only 1.9 square-miles in size, this little city has a high profile for its diverse populace, progressive government, and trendy shopping, dining, and social scenes.

Of the city's current mix of Jews, gays, Russian immigrants, and others, the Jews were the first group to come to the area, spilling west from the Fairfax District where they had settled post-World War II. The gay community was next to discover West Hollywood. Some were attracted by the growing design community here, and others by the relative security of living in this then-unincorporated area in LA County, which was under the jurisdiction of the county sheriff and not the Los Angeles Police Department (said to frequently raid gay clubs). The most recent group to adopt West Hollywood is the Russian immigrant community, many also Jewish, who now comprise 12% of the city's population.

On a stroll through Plummer Park on Santa Monica Boulevard you can see the mosaic of neighbors, who seem to have found a peace, albeit at times uneasy, amongst each other. As an example of how the local government is considerate of its citizenry, West Hollywood was the first U.S. city to declare Yom Kippur (the Jewish New Year) a legal holiday and outlaw discrimination against people with AIDS.

The 37,000 residents enjoy the city's numerous amenities, including rent stabilization, chic shopping and dining, and the beautiful Spanish-style architecture that graces many West Hollywood streets. Santa Monica Boulevard runs the length of the city, and has a business base as diverse as the community itself. On the western end of the street there are many retail stores, cafes, and nightclubs catering to the gay and lesbian community, which is estimated to be anywhere from 25-40% of the city's population. (Check out *Gay USA* by George Hobica for a concise, useful chapter on LA for the gay arrival.) A burgeoning group of gyms and related fitness and beauty businesses have transformed the area near City Hall into Health Row. And further east, the boulevard is home to the entrepreneurial efforts of the thriving Russian-Jewish immigrant community.

West Hollywood is also the site of the Pacific Design Center, a huge collection (1.2 million square feet) of interior design showrooms that anchors a neighborhood of design-related businesses along Melrose Avenue and Beverly and Robertson Boulevards. The Center itself is affectionately known as "The Blue Whale", due to the scale and bright color of the original building. Added later was an equally large, bright green building (Center Green) of more showrooms.

The northernmost part of West Hollywood features some of the most well-known sites on Sunset Boulevard, including nightclubs like The Roxy, The Whiskey, House of Blues, and The Viper Room (now known as the site of River Phoenix's overdose). There's also Sunset Plaza, a tony strip of sidewalk cafes and pricey clothing stores.

Housing in West Hollywood includes lovely, old-style apartments, duplexes, and single-family homes. The city's rent stabilization means that rents can only be raised a predetermined amount each year, and furthermore, even when a unit comes on the market, landlords are restricted by the city's rent board as to the amount the rent can be raised. As a result, there are a number of affordable rentals to be found in West Hollywood.

Area Code: 310.

Zip Code: 90069.

Post Office: West Branch, 820 North San Vicente Boulevard, 652-2345.

Police Department: West Hollywood is contracted with the County of Los Angeles Sheriff's Department, 720 North San Vicente Boulevard, 855-8850.

Emergency Hospital: Cedars-Sinai Medical Center, 8700 Beverly Boulevard, 855-5000.

Library: 715 North San Vicente Boulevard, 652-5340.

Fairfax District (Mid-Wilshire)

Boundaries: North: Willoughby Avenue; **East:** La Brea Avenue; **South:** Pico Boulevard; **West:** La Cienega Boulevard

Long the center of Los Angeles' religious Jewish community, the Fairfax District is now an eclectic blend of cultures, including Indian, Ethiopian, African-American, and urban hip. Indeed, Fairfax Avenue itself is a cultural mish-mash where one can find kosher butchers, Ethiopian restaurants, African artifacts, and Indian spice shops. Even Canter's Delicatessen reflects the diversity of the neighborhood, serving up matzo ball soup to elderly Jewish residents by day, while featuring jazz and blues in the adjoining "Kibitz (Yiddish for "chat") Room" at night.

The Farmer's Market at Fairfax and Third is a favorite for tour bus stops, but Fairfax District locals, too, come for the fresh fruits, vegetables, cafes and butchers. It's also a busy lunch spot for business people, especially the nearby television and movie industry executives (CBS's Television City is right next door).

A retail district is burgeoning along Third Street between La Cienega Boulevard and Crescent Heights, featuring specialty bookstores, cafes, and used and new clothing stores. La Brea Avenue to the east boasts several trendy furniture stores and eateries, and some of the areas prettiest old apartment buildings are along Sycamore Avenue, which is the street just east of La Brea. Finally, there is the famous Melrose Avenue, popularized even more by the successful Fox television series that bears its name, "Melrose Place." Melrose, on the Hollywood border, is LA's funkiest shopping street, and definitely the place to go to find the latest fashions or check out the trendiest food in the city. The street's denizens are some of LA's most urban and cutting-edge, with pierces and tattoos practically de rigueur.

Besides the wonderful mix of local residents in the Fairfax District, the architecture of much of the housing here is another plus. You can find reasonably priced rentals in everything from multi-unit apartment buildings to small houses, but the real gems around here are the older duplexes. Usually two story, with one unit on the top and another below, the area's classic duplexes may feature such nice touches as hardwood floors, built-in cabinetry, leaded or stained glass windows, old-fashioned tiled bathrooms and kitchens, and spacious rooms. It's typical for the landlord to live in one unit and rent out the other, and often the backyard is available for shared access.

Area Code: 213.

Zip Codes: 90035, 90211, 90048, 90036, 90019.

Post Office: Bicentennial Station, 7610 Beverly Boulevard, 933-8448.

Police Districts: (North of Beverly Boulevard) Hollywood Division, 1358 North Wilcox Avenue, 485-4302; (South of Beverly Boulevard) Wilshire Division, 4861 Venice Boulevard, 485-4022.

Emergency Hospitals: Cedars-Sinai Medical Center, 8700 Beverly Boulevard, 310-855-5000; Westside Hospital, 910 South Fairfax Avenue, 213-938-3431.

Library: Fairfax Branch, 161 South Gardner Street, 936-6191.

Hancock Park

Boundaries: North: Melrose Avenue; **East:** Western Avenue; **South:** Wilshire Boulevard; **West:** La Brea Avenue

If you take a quick drive and a cursory look through Hancock Park, you may assume that this neighborhood of stately old houses behind rolling front lawns is simply out of reach for the average LA resident. It's easy to see why, for Hancock Park boasts some of Los Angeles' oldest and grandest homes, including the recently renovated Mayor's mansion, Getty House, on Irving Boulevard. But a closer look at Hancock Park reveals some affordable opportunities for apartments and flats, especially near quaint Larchmont Village and along upper Rossmore. Plus, if the crafts-manship of older buildings appeals to you, much of the housing in this area features classic finishings like hardwood floors and built-in cabinetry.

Larchmont Village, a string of retail businesses and restaurants down Larchmont Avenue, is Los Angeles' answer to Anytown, U.S.A. The small older buildings along the street and general lack of pretension of the stores and cafes are in stark contrast to many of Los Angeles' more trendy neighborhoods, though it still has an upscale feel. No tourist attractions here, Larchmont is truly a neighborhood business district for locals, and features such amenities as florists, dry cleaners, bookstores and eateries.

For those in the housing market, Hancock Park is a place where you can purchase a lovely older home or duplex at much cheaper prices than on the Westside. There is a growing population of Jewish families here, who choose Hancock Park due to its proximity to many conservative and orthodox synagogues.

Area Code: 213.

Zip Code: 90004.

Post Office: Oakwood Station, 265 South Western Avenue, 383-3605.

Police Districts: (North of Beverly Boulevard) Hollywood Division, 1358 North Wilcox Avenue, 485-4310; (South of Beverly Boulevard) Wilshire Division, 4861 Venice Boulevard, 485-4022.

Emergency Hospitals: Queen of Angels Hollywood Presbyterian Medical Center, 1300 North Vermont Avenue, 413-3000; Westside Hospital, 910 South Fairfax Avenue, 938-3431.

Library: Memorial Branch, 4801 Wilshire Boulevard, 934-0855.

Hollywood

Boundaries: North: Mulholland Drive (in the West), Griffith Park (in the East); **East:** Vermont Avenue; **South:** Melrose Avenue; **West:** Laurel Canyon

Hollywood lays out like a geographic hierarchy of the entertainment business, with those who have "made it" living in lovely hillside homes, and those who haven't living below in urban grit. In-between the hills and the flats are a few gentrified bohemian enclaves. One such spot is along Franklin near Tamarind, where on the corner sits a newsstand and a cozy cafe. Tourists come from around the world to see the pink and charcoal terrazzo stars set in the sidewalk on Hollywood Boulevard and Vine Street honoring famous entertainers, yet many visitors are dismayed by the homelessness and crime that exists on the Walk of Fame. Indeed, the promise of fame and fortune lures many to Hollywood, but the realities of hard life in the city have made it a magnet for teenage runaways, drug abusers, and prostitutes.

The Hollywood Hills feature some of Los Angeles' most sought-after residential areas, and many celebrities call the neighborhood home. Also nestled in the Hollywood Hills is the Hollywood Bowl, summer home of the Los Angeles Philharmonic. The summer series includes symphony, pops and jazz, and there are few better ways to spend a warm summer evening than with a picnic and music under the stars at the Bowl.

The area just north of Melrose Avenue features charming, older Spanish style homes, but prices to rent and buy can be high, due to the proximity to the Melrose shops and restaurants. For those willing to brave the above-noted crime, the flats of central Hollywood have their share of beautiful older apartment buildings that still hold some of their original luster. Since many older building don't have garages, parking can be a problem (as well as car theft and vandalism). If it's in your budget, it's probably worthwhile to rent a parking space in the neighborhood if your building doesn't offer one. The population here is an eclectic mix of working class, professional people, Hispanics (53% according to the most recent Census), artists, and aspiring actors.

Area Code: 213.

Zip Codes: 90028, 90068, 90078.

Post Office: Hollywood Station, 1615 North Wilcox Avenue, 464-2194.

Police District: Hollywood Division, 1358 North Wilcox Avenue, 485-4310.

Emergency Hospitals: Kaiser Permanente, 4867 Sunset Boulevard, 667-4011, Queen of Angels Hollywood Presbyterian Medical Center, 1300 North Vermont Avenue, 413-3000; Hollywood Community Hospital, 6245 Delongpre Avenue, 462-2271.

Library: Goldwyn Hollywood Library, 1623 North Ivar Avenue, 467-1821.

Los Feliz/Silverlake/Echo Park

Boundaries: North: Griffith Park; **East:** Golden State Freeway (5) **South:** Hollywood Freeway; **West:** Vermont Avenue

More affordable than the Westside, these are the funky communities that hug the Santa Monica Mountains, between Hollywood and Dodger Stadium. Los Feliz, Silverlake, and Echo Park residents are a mixture of entertainment industry executives, artists and others, including a large gay population.

Los Feliz is the furthest north, and is the closest to Griffith Park, the largest publicly owned park in the United States. The park occupies 4,400 acres in the hills, and features the Los Angeles Zoo, the Griffith Park Observatory Planetarium and Laserium, Travel Town train park, and the Gene Autry Western Heritage Museum. There are also pony rides, tennis courts, a soccer field, merry-go-round, picnic areas, and 50 miles of hiking and horseback riding trails. Los Feliz Village, along Hillhurst Avenue near Franklin Avenue, is the site of several trendy eateries. For a look at the neighborhood's old-style Hollywood mansions, take a ride east of here along Franklin.

Los Feliz seems to blend right into Silverlake further south, and there are several more shopping districts of cafes, antique stores, and bookstores along Vermont Avenue, and along Hyperion Avenue as well. Silverlake's gay enclave seems more low key than that of West Hollywood, and the gay and lesbian residents here are on the whole more into nesting than partying. Further south Silverlake turns into Echo Park, near Dodger Stadium. Echo Park has a sizable Latino population.

All these areas offer close proximity to downtown, although heat and smog are a problem here, especially in the summer. Living options are varied, and include quaint older homes, apartments, and converted (and not so converted) industrial space. Prospective home buyers should know that prices here are reasonable, and architecturally interesting older homes abound. Note that the crime rate in these areas is higher than in other parts of Los Angeles, so be sure to consider the security of your housing and parking if you want to live here.

Area Code: 213.

Zip Code: 90026.

Post Office: Edendale Station, 1525 North Alvarado, 413-3838.

Police District: Northeast Division, 3353 San Fernando Drive, 485-2563.

Emergency Hospitals: Children's Hospital, 4650 Sunset Boulevard, 660-2450; Queen of Angels Hollywood Presbyterian Medical Center, 1300 North Vermont Avenue, 413-3000.

Libraries: Los Feliz Branch, 1939 1/2 Hillhurst Avenue, 664-2903; Echo Park Branch, 515 North Laveta Terrace, 350-7808.

Leimert Park

Boundaries: North: Martin Luther King Jr. Boulevard; **East:** Leimert Boulevard, **South:** Vernon Avenue; **West:** Crenshaw Boulevard

Nestled in the Crenshaw District is Leimert Park, one of the first planned communities in Los Angeles. Development here began in the early 1930's and grew around the park itself (located at the triangular intersection of Leimert and Crenshaw), created by Olmsted & Olmsted, a later incarnation of the same firm that designed New York's Central Park. The surrounding area of shops, 1940's-style duplexes, and houses on wide, tree-lined streets is known as Leimert Park Village.

Once a middle-class white neighborhood, Leimert Park now reflects the composition of the surrounding Crenshaw District, which, according the 1990 census figures, is 83% African American. Leimert Park itself is home to the African Americans with the highest per capita income in Los Angeles, reflected in the lovely homes and well-maintained streets that distinguish this middle-class neighborhood.

Most notably, Leimert Park has become a hub of activity for Black culture, music, and heritage—it is perhaps the Los Angeles neighborhood most firmly rooted in Afrocentrism. Stroll down Degnan Boulevard and you will find galleries, art centers, jazz clubs and bookstores, all highlighting African American themes. An annual jazz festival here draws music lovers from all over the city, though security is still a problem in this evolving neighborhood.

Homes and rentals here are less expensive that on the Westside, and often boast 1930's and 40's architectural features not found in many other parts of the city like West LA. For example, the local city council member's office estimates that a vintage two-bedroom duplex in Leimert Park might rent for $825, while a comparable unit on the Westside would cost upwards of $1,300. Since Leimert Park is located just seven miles southwest of Downtown, the commute for Downtown workers is fairly easy.

Area Code: 213.

Zip Code: 90008.

Post Office: Crenshaw Station, 3894 Crenshaw Boulevard, 295-3133.

Police District: Southwest Division, 1546 West Martin Luther King Jr. Boulevard, 485-2582.

Emergency Hospitals: University of Southern California (USC) Medical Center, 1200 North State Street, 226-2622; Daniel Freeman Memorial Hospital, 333 North Prairie Avenue, 674-7050.

Libraries: Angeles Mesa Branch, 2700 West 52nd Street, 292-4328; View Park County Library, 3854 West 54th Street, 293-5371.

Downtown

Boundaries: North: 101 Freeway; **East:** Santa Ana Freeway; **South:** Santa Monica Freeway (10); **West:** Harbor Freeway

While most people think of Downtown as a place to commute to, not a place to live, parts of Downtown contain new condominium high-rises, as well as artists-in-residence and loft-type housing. Downtown living offers close proximity to many of the city's finest cultural institutions including the Arata Isozaki-designed Museum of Contemporary Art (MOCA) and The Music Center, as well as the recently-renovated central library and its outstanding gardens. There's also easy access to a smattering of ethnic hamlets tucked amidst the financial towers, like the Mexican village-style Olvera Street, Chinatown, and Little Tokyo. Just south of Downtown are several work/live artists studios, such as the large Santa Fe Art Colony at 2401 South Santa Fe, and The Brewery at 1920 North Main Street.

In 1993, Los Angeles opened the first phase of a long-awaited subway, the Metro Red Line. Starting at the beautiful, historic Union Station on North Alameda Street, residents can now ride through most of Downtown in seven minutes. Eventually, the line will extend to Hollywood and the San Fernando Valley, and already the Blue Line light rail transports passengers from Downtown to Long Beach.

It is important to note that crime and urban grit are as much a part of downtown living here as in any city. Since Downtown LA really clears out at night, some areas can have an almost abandoned feeling after dark.

Area Code: 213.

Zip Codes: 90012—15, 90017, 90057.

Post Office: Terminal Annex, 900 North Alameda, 617-4404.

Police District: Central Division, 251 East 6th Street, 485-3294.

Emergency Hospitals: Good Samaritan Hospital, 616 South Witmer, 977-2121; White Memorial Medical Center, 1720 Brooklyn Avenue, 268-5000; University of Southern California (USC) Medical Center, 1200 North State Street, 226-2622.

Libraries: Central Library, 630 West 5th Street, 612-3200; Little Tokyo Branch, 600 East Third Street, 612-0525; Chinatown Branch, 536 West College Street, 620-0925.

Transportation: Metro Red Line Information, 800-2LA-RIDE.

Pasadena

Boundaries: North: Montana Street (in the West), Washington Boulevard (in the East); **East:** West of Michilinda Avenue; **South:** Columbia Street (in the West), California Boulevard (in the East); **West:** Hills West of Linda Vista Avenue

Pasadena's claim to fame is the always-sunny New Year's Day Tournament of Roses Parade and Rose Bowl, but this city's roots, like much of the Valley, are in agriculture. Pioneers who came to this area in the late 1800's found success farming oranges and olives, and named their community Pasadena, derived from two Chippewa Indian words meaning "Crown of the Valley."

By the turn of the century the town had become a winter retreat for wealthy Midwesterners such as David B. Gamble of Proctor & Gamble and chewing gum magnate William Wrigley Jr. Through the next several decades, it was known as a quiet, pretty, conservative place to raise a family.

Over the past few years, a revitalized "old town" has sparked new interest in the area. Colorado Boulevard is Pasadena's main artery, and the heart of "Old Pasadena." The city's original business district, Old Pasadena is bounded by Pasadena Avenue, Walnut Street, Arroyo Parkway and Green Street, and the renovated historic buildings now offer a unique array of retail stores, art galleries, movie theaters, antique shops, restaurants, and offices.

This reborn downtown, along with the city's other plusses, have sparked the interest of many singles and young families who are moving to Pasadena. The city's carefully preserved historic residential architecture is a lure to people who appreciate the classic Craftsman homes so prevalent here. In addition, Pasadena residents like the small town atmosphere, coupled with first-rate cultural institutions like the Norton Simon Museum, which features Western European painting and Asian sculpture, and the Huntington Library and Gardens, which features fine art, rare manuscripts, and a lovely botanical garden.

Depending on where you work, Pasadena can be an easy commute (to Downtown Los Angeles or parts of the Valley) or a long haul. On a clear day, its scenic location nestled in the foothills of the San Gabriel Mountains is spectacular. Unfortunately, more often the inverse is true, and Pasadena can have some of Southern California's hottest and smoggiest weather, during which the nearby mountains are not even visible.

Area Code: 818.

Zip Codes: 91109—9.

Post Office: 600 Lincoln Avenue, 304-7122.

Police Department: Pasadena is served by its own municipal police force. Headquarters: 207 North Garfield Avenue, 405-4550.

Emergency Hospitals: Huntington Memorial Hospital, 100 Congress Street, 397-5000; Las Encinas Hospital, 2900 E. Del Mar Boulevard, 795-9901; St. Luke's Medical Center, 2632 East Washington Boulevard, 797-1141.

Libraries: Main Library, 285 East Walnut Street, 405-4052; County Sunnyslope Library, 346 South Rosemead Boulevard, 792-5733.

San Fernando Valley

The San Fernando Valley is so vast that covering it well would require a separate guide book. Therefore, what follows is a short history of the area, and brief mentions of some of the neighborhoods.

The Valley began as a farming and ranching community, famous for its oranges, lemons, walnuts and persimmons. But by the mid 1900's, it became a bastion of white suburbia. After World War II, "the Valley," as it's known, looked like a working model for the American Dream as housing tracts cropped up everywhere offering Los Angelenos affordable homes complete with two-car garages and a patch of lawn to call their own.

Now, nearly four-million people live in the Valley, and while some residents of the city side have disdain for its suburban feel (this is, after all, home of the much-maligned "Valley Girl"), the Valley offers cheaper, more laid-back living options, and a closer proximity to many businesses, including the entertainment studios and related businesses in **Burbank, Glendale** and **Universal City**. In addition, home buyers find that they can get a lot more house for their money in the Valley, and while the temperatures are hotter and the smog worse, the 'burbs lifestyle is just what some people are seeking. In addition, this formerly white enclave has taken on a more multi-ethnic flavor in recent years, due to an influx of African American, Asian and Latino residents.

Ventura Boulevard runs through the southern portion of the Valley, and is a thriving business and restaurant strip. It also serves to mark the more prestigious neighborhoods, those "south of the Boulevard," from the more moderate homes on the other side. **Encino** (the most exclusive area in this part of the Valley), **Sherman Oaks,** and **Van Nuys** are family-oriented neighborhoods of middle and upper-income residents, and consist mostly of single-family houses and condominiums. **Studio City**, so named because the area was a hub for filming activity during the silent film era in the 1920's, contains mostly single-family homes in the hilly areas, and some apartments and condominiums on the most heavily traveled streets. Nearby **North Hollywood** is home to the Academy of Television Arts and Sciences, bestowers of the Emmy Awards. Like Studio City, it is a family- oriented community of single-family homes, with some apartments and condominiums. All of these communities are part of the city of Los Angeles.

The West Valley has seen much growth in the past few years, and continues to be a hot spot for new development. Planned (and often gated) communities in areas such as **Agoura, Westlake Village, Calabasas** and **Thousand Oaks** have attracted young families who feel safer and can afford more in these clean, secluded neighborhoods, as well as others who want out of LA's city life. The commute is long for those who work in Los Angeles proper, but the suburban lifestyle is substantially different from most neighborhoods in the city, and that's preferable to the West Valley residents.

The Northridge earthquake of 1994 caused much damage to the Valley, especially around **Northridge** itself and other scattered locations like parts of Sherman Oaks. Now the only marks that remain from the quake are the rebuilding efforts, and local merchants' fears about the quake causing "ghost towns" in hard hit areas appear to have been unfounded.

FINDING an apartment in the Los Angeles area can be very simple or very difficult, depending on where you are looking. (The neighborhood guides at the beginning of this book indicate in which areas it is most difficult to find housing.) First, determine how much money you are willing to spend on your monthly rent, and how big an apartment you want. If you need a two-bedroom place but can only afford $600 per month, there's no need to look in Beverly Hills.

Once you have determined your rent budget and size needs, if time permits, take a walk or drive through the neighborhoods in which you would like to live. Not only will this give you a feel for the areas, but often you can find "For Rent" signs by thoroughly combing the streets that interest you.

Finally, ask around. Co-workers and friends may know of vacancies in their buildings, and landlords are often more willing to take a referral from a trustworthy tenant, rather than bring in a stranger off the street.

Here are some other ways to find your new digs:

Newspaper Classified Advertisements

Another key resource for would-be renters is classified advertisements. The Sunday **Los Angeles Times** lists pages of rentals, as do the smaller regional and weekly alternative newspapers like the **LA Weekly** and the **Santa Monica Outlook**. (Here's a sneaky tip: many grocery stores get an abridged version of the Sunday *Los Angeles Times*, including the classified ads, on Saturday nights. So, if you grab a copy on Saturday, you can plot your Sunday apartment hunt and be a little ahead of the pack.) You can also pick up a copy of the **Apartment Guide** covering Los Angeles and the San Fernando Valley. The *Apartment Guide* is a free monthly directory of apartment listings, and is available at Von's grocery stores, 7-Eleven stores, Stop 'N Go, AM-PM Mini Markets, and other convenience stores, motels and hotels, real estate agents, banks, moving companies, schools and airports. If despite these many locations you cannot find one, the *Apartment Guide* is located in Van Nuys and can be reached at (818) 893-1249. Another similar publication is the **Apartment Magazine,** also free of charge and available at major supermarkets, convenience stores, visitor centers, and street racks.

Bulletin Boards

Many neighborhood coffee shops, grocery stores, and other similar places (for instance, One Life health food store on Main Street at the border between Venice and Santa Monica) have bulletin boards or wall space devoted to posting neighborhood announcements. Tucked between flyers for yoga classes and dog walkers, you may find notices of apartment or house rentals. More often, you'll find flyers for apartment shares, which is another option to consider, especially if you want to live in a popular area.

Rental Agents

Using a rental or real estate agency is not the norm here, and is most common for people trying to locate high-end apartments, or apartments in an area with few vacancies, like Santa Monica. Since real estate agents help locate only apartments listed with agencies, the landlord pays the fees, so there is no cost to you. On the other hand, apartment finding rental agencies require a fee from you before you can view their listings. It is unlikely that cheap rent-controlled units come into the hands of real estate agents, because owners seldom want to pay an extra fee since the rent is already low, and such units move quickly by word of mouth. Nonetheless, if you are not terribly price-conscious or need assistance landing a rental in a specific neighborhood, you might want to call a real estate agent or sign up with an apartment finding service.

The biggest real estate agencies in the Los Angeles area are **The Prudential•Jon Douglas, Coldwell Banker**, and **Fred Sands**. They have offices all over the city, so check the phone book and call the one in the neighborhood in which you want to live.

Two apartment finding services to check out are **Rent Time** (213-655-5949) and **Rentline** (310-789-RENT). Or, for a fee of $400, **PRM Relocation** (800-522-6863) will help you locate an apartment. This firm uses the resources that are available to anyone such as classified ads and real estate agencies, but it may be a good choice for people relocating from out of state or those with the money to pay someone else to do their leg work.

On the Hunt

When you actually check out a prospective apartment, here are some guidelines:

- While it is not necessary to wear your Sunday best, good grooming impresses landlords and apartment managers as much as it impresses the rest of us. Landlords are looking for responsible tenants who will pay their rent on time each month, and take good care of their unit. Try to look the part.
- Come with checkbook in hand. Often the person who is willing to put down a deposit first will get the apartment.
- Have ready access to your references, both credit and personal.
- Check the appliances and the water pressure. Often apartments in Los Angeles do not come with refrigerators, and you may need to buy or rent your own. Some landlords offer rentals on refrigerators they have in the building.
- Are there water stains on the ceiling? That's a possible sign of past leaks.
- How did the building fare in the last earthquake? Superficial cracks along the walls or ceiling don't necessarily indicate a serious structural problem. The city's building inspector office can provide you with information if you are unsure.
- Is there secured parking? How many spaces? If two, are they tandem (so that one car blocks the other) or side by side? Is there an extra fee for parking?
- Are there laundry facilities in the building?
- Are you responsible for paying gas, water, and/or electricity? This policy varies from place to place and paying any combination or none at all are both possible.
- If possible, talk with a few tenant to see if they like the building, landlord, location, etc.

Leases, Security Deposits and Rent Control

In most cases, leases and security deposits fall under the jurisdiction of state law. If you have any questions regarding your lease, security deposit, or rent control, contact your rent stabilization board. The numbers are listed below.

The lease is a legally binding contract, which outlines both your obligations to your landlord, and your landlord's obligations to you. Of course, you should read your lease very carefully, and get a full written explanation for anything that does not make sense to you.

Here are some things to consider in your lease:

- Is this a month-to-month lease, one-year, or longer?

• Are you allowed pets?
• Are you allowed water beds?
• Can you sublet your apartment?
• Are you allowed to barbecue on the property?
• Can you sublet your unit?

Under California state law, in most instances the security deposit cannot exceed two months rent for an unfurnished unit or three months rent for a furnished unit. The deposit can be collected in addition to the first month's rent. In some cities, for instance in West Hollywood, landlords are required to pay interest on your security deposit. Again, check with your rent board.

Rent Stabilization

Several cities in the Los Angeles area have enacted rent stabilization, in an effort to offer affordable rental housing. Rent control laws and their effects can vary according to city, but a recently enacted state law has made most cities' rent control laws similar across the state, and profoundly altered the laws in Santa Monica (see section entitled "Santa Monica" under "Neighborhoods" chapter). For the most up-to-date information, contact the following rent stabilization boards to learn how rent control works in your area:

• **Beverly Hills Rent Office**
  455 North Rexford Drive, 310-285-1031
• **Los Angeles Department of Housing**
  200 North Spring Street, 213-847-7833
• **Santa Monica Rent Control Board**
  1685 Main Street, Room 202, 310-458-8751
• **West Hollywood Department of Rent Stabilization**
  8611 Santa Monica Boulevard, 310-854-7450

As the 1980's band Missing Persons sang, "Nobody walks in LA." They drive. Los Angeles is famous for its "car culture," and with good reason. The city of Los Angeles covers 467 square miles, and while it is technically possible to get around by foot, bicycle, bus, and the new **Metro** light rail or subway, in most cases it is quicker and more convenient to drive.

The Air Quality Management District (AQMD) is doing its best to encourage use of public transportation, carpooling, bicycling and walking, and many smog-conscious residents are trying to cut down on their driving, especially during peak commute hours. (There's even a hot line that you can call, 1-800-CUT-SMOG, to report a vehicle that you see emitting exhaust for more than ten seconds.) In addition, the AQMD has mandated that companies with one hundred or more employees must encourage smog-cutting transportation alternatives. In consideration of these mandates, some companies now operate on "flex time," which allows employees to work a compressed schedule of nine out of ten working days so that fewer cars are on the road. Nonetheless, the bottom line is that even though you may want to limit your driving, like most people here, you probably want to have a car.

Buying a Car

Buying a car can be exciting, a hassle, and an expense. New cars may be purchased or leased through dealers; automobile dealers are listed in the telephone directory. Used cars can be purchased through dealers as well, or through the classified advertisements in local newspapers. Or, you can go to a newsstand and pick up a copy of the *Auto Trader* (800-395-SELL), a publication of advertisements for used cars along with photos of the vehicles. Beware that while the prices in the paper or Auto Trader may look cheaper than through dealers, there is often no warranty on cars that you buy via the want ads. It's a good idea to take the used car you are thinking about purchasing to a mechanic, and pay him/her to look the vehicle over before you buy it.

Once you know the cost of your new car, your expenses aren't over. In the state of California, it is illegal to drive an uninsured automobile. Now for the bad news: Los Angeles has some of the highest automobile insurance rates in the state. In fact, according to a 1995 Runzheimer International survey, it costs more to own and operate a car in Los Angeles than it does in any other metropolitan area in the U.S. The best advice is to call around to many insurance companies and get quotes before you buy your car.

For most auto-related information, including insurance, emergency road service, and travel services, you may find it worth the $58 annual membership fee to join the **Automobile Club of Southern California**, the regional branch of the **American Automobile Association (AAA)**. They are located at:

Burbank, 550 North 3rd Street, 818-843-2833.
Culver City, 4512 South Sepulveda Boulevard, 310-390-9866.
Hollywood, 4773 Hollywood Boulevard, 213-666-2420.
Inglewood, 1234 Centinela Avenue, 310-673-5170.
Los Angeles (Downtown), 2601 South Figueroa Street, 213-741-3111.
Manhattan Beach, 700 South Aviation Boulevard, 310-376-0521.
Pasadena, 801 East Union Street, 818-795-0601.
West Los Angeles, 1900 South Sepulveda Boulevard, 310-914-8500.

Anti-theft Devices

Newcomers to Los Angeles are often struck by the frequent din of car alarms. Unfortunately, these annoying devices are felt to be a necessity by many residents, since LA is a global hot spot for car theft. The reasons are many. For starters, Los Angelenos' cars are known to be a little nicer and more well-kept that those in other parts of the country, and there are simply more cars per capita here than in other regions. Also, our proximity to an international border and a major port mean that stolen vehicles can be disposed of more quickly than in the Midwest or other regions.

For these reasons, the Automobile Club of Southern California recommends anti-theft devices. The general feeling is that although few mechanisms will stop a professional car thief determined to take your car, devices do thwart amateurs. If you decide to buy an anti-theft device, be sure to tell your automobile insurer, as they often offer discounts for car owners who have them on their vehicles. Here are a few for you to consider:

• Steering wheel locks are one of the cheapest ways to go. While a pro can break through them with ease, they may be a deterrent to the thief looking for an easy target. Some locks go around the steer-

ing column only, while others hook around the gas pedal to the
steering wheel.

• Audible car alarms can scare amateurs, and the blinking light inside
your car that accompanies many of these systems may be enough
to make a thief choose someone else's car to steel. However,
sometimes these alarms are set too sensitively and thus tend to go
off easily, and the California Vehicle Code allows police to tow and
impound an unattended vehicle after its siren has blared for 45 minutes. These systems range in cost from $100 to $500, and are
sold at car dealers, or from auto parts and electronics shops.

• Kill switches can be installed to shut down your car's starter, fuel
pump, or ignition, unless the switch is first disengaged by the
motorist. Auto parts stores sell the devices, and a mechanic will
have to install it for you.

• The most high-end systems are those like Lojack and Teletrac,
which install transmitters in your car. Lojack systems are tracked by
police cars with homing devices, while Teletrac does the tracking
itself and then tells police where to look for your vehicle. Both systems have excellent recovery rates (about 90%) and cost about
$500-600 for installation.

• Finally, here's a free option that can be effective. More than 100
Southern California cities offer a system called Combat Auto Theft
(CAT) through local police departments. A CAT decal on your car
authorizes police to stop your vehicle for no other reason than
seeing the decal if the car is on the streets between the hours of
1-5 a.m.

Auto Safety

Safety experts say that with the advent of car alarms and other anti-theft
devices, autos are getting more difficult to steal. Unfortunately, thieves
who formerly would steal unattended parked cars are now finding that
violent confrontation, i.e. carjacking, may be the only way to get the cars
they want. Here are some guidelines for auto safety:

• Know how to get to where you are going. Study your route ahead of
time to eliminate the need to look at a map while driving.

• Keep car doors locked while driving, and keep windows up in unfa-
miliar areas. If it is hot and you have no air conditioning, roll down
the window enough to get air in the car, but not enough for an arm
to get in.

• Keep your wallet or purse hidden, either under the seat or in
the trunk.

• Park in well-lit areas. If you need to use a pay phone or purchase
gasoline, stop where the attendants can see you. Having someone
pump gas for you is less dangerous (but more expensive) than getting out of your car and pumping and paying yourself.

• Do not be tricked into getting out of your car. If you are rear-ended in a remote or dark area and feel uneasy about getting out of your car to exchange insurance information, motion to the other driver to follow you to a police or fire station, or a 24-hour store.
• Do not stop for flashing white lights. Law enforcement vehicles use red flashers or blue and white ones.
• Drive in the middle lane if you feel insecure in a certain area. Try not to get into a lane where you can easily be cut off. If a car blocks you intentionally, honk repeatedly for help, but do not get out of your car.
• Most importantly, if the worst happens and you are confronted, give up your car, your jewelry, your wallet or purse. Often violence occurs when citizens resist a carjacking or mugging. No possession is more valuable than your life.

Remember, in general, driving in and around Los Angeles is not a dangerous proposition. Millions of people do it every day, without confrontation or even a hint of danger. Defensive, alert driving is still one of the best ways to get around in LA.

Thomas Guides

Thomas Guides are loose-leaf books of detailed Los Angeles neighborhood road maps, and for the new LA driver, your Thomas Guide may be your Bible. Most people have a well-worn copy of a Thomas Guide thrown in their trunk or back seat, because in a city this large, you never know when you will need to figure out how to get from here to there.

Thomas Guides can be purchased at most local bookstores for $15–$30.

F OR THE past few years, when you flipped on the televised national
news there always seemed to be some drama occurring in LA.
Riots, earthquakes, fires, landslides, floods, or captivating
trials–there was Southern California in the starring role. Well the
riots are long over (though not the social issues that spawned them), the
trials will probably keep coming (the Menendez brothers, Heidi Fleiss,
O.J. Simpson, who's next?), but the one thing you can bet on as a part
of life here is natural disasters.

Fortunately, most natural disasters like earthquakes, fires, landslides, and floods happen infrequently and seriously effect relatively few
people. While you may be inconvenienced by increased traffic due to
flooding or a temporary loss of power due to a temblor, the vast majority
of LA residents have suffered no loss of property or bodily injury due to
these disasters. On the other hand, for those few people who are vic-
tims, the results can be devastating. While most locals do not go through
life in fear of these disasters, it is wise to have a healthy respect for
Mother Nature's power, and, when possible take precautions to guard
against it.

Earthquakes

One of the biggest fears people relate about living in California is earthquakes. While most natives aren't too frightened by the swaying or
bumps of small temblors, no one relishes the thought of the proverbial
"Big One."

The 6.6 Northridge earthquake that rocked LA on January 17, 1994
killed 57 people, with 1,500 more suffering serious injuries. It is believed
that casualties would have been much greater had it struck in the middle
of the day, when the collapsed stores would have been filled with shoppers and the failed freeways crowded with cars. (However, most earthquakes occur at night) 22,000 people were forced to leave their homes

(either permanently or while repairs were made) due to quake damage, and more than 3,000 buildings were declared unsafe for reentry. Yet, when you consider the millions of people who felt the quake that early morning, the number of people affected in more than a casual way was relatively small.

While only chance dictates who will be in the wrong place at the wrong time during a quake, there are precautions you can take to aid your survival in an earthquake. Here are some for your to consider.

In your home:
- Place your bed away from windows and bookshelves, and don't hang heavy objects nearby.
- Heavy ceiling fans and lights should be supported with a cable bolted to the ceiling joist. The cable should have enough slack to allow it to sway.
- Store flashlights and batteries in your bedroom.
- In an accessible closet, store: a battery-powered radio, extra flashlights and batteries, candles and matches, money, medical supplies, canned or dehydrated food, sleeping bags, a 1-gallon container of water, matches, and   sturdy shoes. Water and food should be changed for freshness every six months. Local home improvement stores sell earthquake preparedness kits containing some of these items.
- Store heavy objects in lower shelves.
- Use brackets to bolt bookshelves, file cabinets, and other heavy pieces of furniture to the walls. Be sure to connect brackets to wall studs.
- Brace chimneys. (Usually a professional will need to do this for you.)
- Fasten down lamps and valuable objects, and use putty to hold breakables in place.
- Be sure your home is bolted to its foundation. This is especially a concern with older homes, many of which were not fastened to the foundation at the time of construction.
- Strap your water heater to the wall.
- Put latches on cabinet doors.
- Know where your water and gas valves are located, and how to shut them off.

In your car:
- Store the following: flashlight, batteries, portable battery-powered radio, first aid kit, maps, food such as trail mix or non-melting energy bars, water, tools, and cash.

In your office:
- Store the following: a portable battery-powered radio, flashlight with spare batteries, and a first aid kit. Most companies have emergency procedures in place to follow in the event of an emergency.

When an earthquake strikes:

• At the risk of stating the obvious or the seemingly impossible, remain calm. You can cause more needless disruption by irrational behavior than the earthquake itself may produce for you.

• Move away from windows and heavy objects that may tumble.

• If the shaking is severe, stand in a door jam, or crawl beneath a sturdy piece of furniture like a desk.

• Falling or sparking power lines present a danger, so think twice before running outside.

• If you smell gas after a quake, turn off your gas valves and notify authorities that you may have a leak.

• Your electrical power may be disrupted.

• Cordless telephones that run on electricity will not work if the power is down, so it's a good idea to have at least one phone that doesn't require electricity to work. Phone service may be disrupted, but often it is the high volume of calls within the quake area that causes overloads of the telephone lines. If you do have service, make only necessary calls. True emergency telephone calls may have a difficult time connecting because local people are calling around town to check on friends. Instead, designate a friend or family member outside the area (preferably out of state) who can serve as the point person to your circle of friends. Since calls to and from outside the area are often easier to make, your point person can keep track of who is okay and report to concerned family members and friends, thus saving vital phone lines.

• Remember, most earthquakes are over in a matter of seconds. However, you can expect aftershocks, sometimes strong ones, for weeks or months after a quake.

Fires, Landslides, and Floods

Summer brush fires are a normal occurrence in California, especially in hilly canyon areas with a good deal of vegetation. If you live in such an area (for instance Malibu, Topanga Canyon, or other canyons), be sure to clear the brush around your home before the summer dry season.

Following are recommendations from wildfire specialists on how to shield your home, especially in areas of high fire danger:

• Get rid of a wood shake or shingle roof, and replace it with a steel or composition roof rated Class A (will not burn) or Class B (slightly less protective).

• Reduce or eliminate shrubbery that would act as fuel in your yard and along your driveway. Remove "torch trees" close to your home, trim flammable, dead branches from older trees, and maintain thirty feet or more of "defensive space" in the form of protective landscaping around your home and one hundred feet or more downhill.

The U.S. Forest Service or National Park Service can provide you with information on protective landscaping.
- Be certain that your community has roads that are clear of vegetation within at least twenty feet on either side, to act as a firebreak and allow for safe evacuation and access by fire fighting equipment.

Burn areas are especially vulnerable to landslides in the rainy season, as the vegetation that normally holds the hills in place has been burnt away. But fire sites are not the only places that landslides occur. The sharp cliffs above the Pacific Coast Highway regularly slide during the rains, and slides are also common in all hilly neighborhoods. Residents often use sandbags to shore up iffy areas, and tarps to cover precarious hillsides.

These same neighborhoods are particularly susceptible to flooding. Remote canyon roads may be inaccessible during heavy rains, though not for longer than a few days.

Note that massive fires, landslides, and floods are seldom issues for people living in the most populated areas of Los Angeles.

O NE OF the first things you will need to do in Los Angeles is settle your banking and other financial needs. Every major national and many international financial institutions have branches in Los Angeles, so shop around for what suits your needs.

Banking

Many banks have offices all over the city, so that while your main branch may be near your home, there is likely to be an ATM near your office, as well. **Bank of America** and **Wells Fargo Bank** are the two largest banks on the West Coast, and the numerous branches each bank offers can be convenient. However, with these large institutions, the days of knowing your teller and personalized service seem remote. Then again, with the advent of direct deposit paychecks, ATMs (automated teller machine), and computerized telephone systems for checking your balance and finding out when your checks clear, some bank customers never find the need to actually walk into their branch.

If you want to go truly high-tech, manage your money on-line, and participate in home-banking, you'll need to call around and determine which banks offer service hookups to your home banking software system. Microsoft's Money program and Intuit's Quicken are the most popular home-banking programs, but so far, only a small percentage of banking customers use these programs. In the future, however, more and more people will be paying bills, balancing checkbooks, transferring funds and looking for loans on-line. As evidence, Wells Fargo Bank already offers its customers account information on the Internet.

Many smaller institutions such as **Santa Monica Bank** and **Coast Federal Bank** are trying to compete with the big corporations by offering no or fewer fees, free checks, and other customer services. The best advice is to look around before you settle on a bank.

Checking and Savings Accounts

Many establishments will not take your check unless it is local and imprinted with your name, address and telephone number. Needless to say, it helps to get your checking account set up as soon as possible. Account services, fees and interest payments vary according to how much money you keep in your account, what services you require, and how many accounts you open with the bank.

A few businesses will only take checks numbered higher than 500 or 1,000 (indicating an established account), but you can get around this by asking your bank to start your checks at a number higher than 1. While everyone now uses ATMs, some local grocery stores allow you to pay for your groceries with your ATM card, automatically debiting the cost of your groceries from your checking account. Also, many employers now offer direct deposit, wherein your account is credited with your paycheck amount on payday without you making a deposit. Some banks offer a monthly credit for direct deposit, since it saves the bank time and paper.

Most banks offer savings accounts linked to your checking account. As with checking accounts, services, fees and interest rates vary.

If you have moved to Los Angeles from another U.S. city and previously banked with a large national institution with offices here, chances are you can simply transfer your account to a new home office in LA with greater ease than starting a new account at another bank.

Credit Cards

Credit card applications are available in most stores and banks, or you can call to obtain one.

American Express offers both traditional "charge cards", wherein there is no credit extended and you must pay your entire bill each month, as well as actual credit cards. To apply for an American Express Card, call 800-528-4800.

Diner's Club Card costs $80, and is designed for people who travel a great deal, either for business or pleasure. They have a generous frequent flyer mileage program. To apply for a Diner's Club Card, call 800-234-6377.

Discover Cards/Private Issue Cards can be obtained by calling 800-347-2683. There is no annual fee for the Discover Card, and the annual fee for the Private Issue Card is $40.

MasterCards and VISA Cards can be obtained through banks, university alumni associations, credit unions, and other financial institutions. Many people are choosing to align their MasterCard or VISA with a charity or airline frequent traveler program, whereby every dollar that you charge gives either a percentage to that charity, or points toward free travel.

Department Stores in Los Angeles also offer their own store credit cards, although most department stores will take local personal checks with proper identification or major credit cards. The advantages of having a store credit card include advance notice of sales and often no annual fee.

Discount Dining Cards

A recent trend is the use of discount dining cards, which offer up to 25% off your dining bills at selected restaurants. Many of LA's best-known restaurants participate. Here are two of the most frequently used dining cards, and how they work:

Transmedia advances cash to restaurants in exchange for food and beverage credits, which are in turn marketed to card members. When members dine at participating restaurants, they sign a Transmedia charge slip, and add a tip, just like with any credit card. The bill is charged directly onto their Visa, MasterCard, or Discover account, with an offsetting credit equal to 25% of the food and beverage portion of the check. Every six weeks members receive revised directories, which list hundreds of restaurants in the United States, United Kingdom, and Australia. The annual subscriber fee is $50; Transmedia's toll-free number is 800-422-5090.

Premier Dining Card offers two for one discounts at more than 9,000 restaurants across the country. Or, for solo dining, some affiliated eateries offer 50% off one entree. Like Transmedia, the Premier card is linked to your regular credit card. For those times when you're out of town on business, Premier offers a toll-free number to call and find out the closest restaurants that honor their card. The Premier Dining Card has a $49 annual membership fee; for information call 800-346-3241.

Your credit card company may offer discounts on dining at selected restaurants. For example, Diner's Club offers to their card holders 20% off the entire restaurant bill when dining at one of the 900 participating restaurants through their LeCard program, and the **J. C. Penny National Bank Visa Card** offers 25% off the food bill for one to four people In selected hotel restaurants.

Income Taxes

Federal income tax forms may be obtained in the lobby of the **Federal Building,** 11000 Wilshire Boulevard, Westwood, 310-477-6565, or at your local post office or library.

State income tax forms can be obtained from the state **Franchise Tax Board** office, 300 South Spring Street, downtown, or by calling 800-852-5711. The Franchise Tax Board office is open from 8 a.m. - 5 p.m., Monday through Friday. As with federal forms, your local post office or library may have state forms, as well.

There is no city income tax for residents of Los Angeles, Beverly Hills, Culver City, West Hollywood, Malibu or Santa Monica.

O KAY. You've found an apartment, signed a lease, perhaps bought a car, and established a checking account. Here are some of the folks to whom you will be writing those first checks. The following covers most of the services you will need to start up the necessities in your home: light, water, gas, telephone, and that modern almost-necessity, cable television. There is also automobile-related information here, as well as a few other tidbits.

Southern California Gas Company

Those of you with all-electric houses or apartments can skip this section.

Many places have gas cooking ranges, and some places have gas heat and/or gas fireplaces. To get your gas service started, call The Gas Company. Check the telephone directory for the telephone number, as they differ depending on where you live.

If you have only a gas cooking range, your monthly bills should not be more than $10. If you have gas heat, your bills during the winter will be slightly higher than during the summer, but remember, it seldom goes below 45 degrees here, so your heating bills should not be a major part of your budget.

Southern California Edison

Southern California Edison provides electricity to Culver City, Santa Monica, Inglewood, and portions of Marina del Rey and Manhattan Beach. To find out if So Cal Ed services your home or to start new service, call 310-204-4030. Residents of the beach communities will find less need for air conditioners (and may not have one at all) than those further east or in the Valley.

City of Los Angeles Department of Water and Power (and other water companies)

Commonly called the **DWP,** this municipal office serves electricity and water to the majority of Los Angeles. For new service, call 800-342-5397.

Electricity bills vary depending on usage. The big energy-users during the summer are air conditioners, so beware.

(For an interesting fictionalized account of the history of this powerful government office, view the movie "Chinatown ", with Jack Nicholson. It tells the story of how early Los Angeles officials secured water rights for the city during its boom years. The main character, "Hollis Mulwray", is a thinly-veiled reference to William Mulholland, a turn-of-the-century water engineer who is now remembered by the 22-mile skyline highway on the crest of the Santa Monica Mountains that bears his name.)

Santa Monica has its own city department of water, reachable at 310-458-8224. Culver City's water is run by the **Southern California Water Company,** at 310-838-2143. Malibu is served by the **Las Virgenes Municipal Water Company,** 818-880-4110, and the **Los Angeles County Water District #29,** 310-456-6621.

GTE

Some parts of Los Angeles receive local telephone service via **GTE,** others through **Pacific Bell,** though local service in the Los Angeles area will be opened to competition in the near future. In the meantime, generally, GTE serves Malibu, Mar Vista, Marina del Rey, Pacific Palisades, Playa del Rey, Santa Monica, Topanga, Venice and portions of Brentwood and Culver City. To begin new service, call 800-482-7709. For billing information, call 800-223-6177.

When you begin new service, standard charges for installing and re-arranging telephone service apply. For a complete listing of the many service options available, check the front of the *GTE Everything Pages*, or call for a brochure.

Here in LA there is such a thing as "local long distance calls." For example, expect to pay for most calls outside your area code, even if you live in 310 and are calling only a few blocks away to 213. Due to the extremely high volume of telephone usage in the Los Angeles area (i.e. new phones, faxes, modems, and cellulars), two additional area codes will be overlayed into preexisting codes. In the 818 area (San Fernando Valley), the new code will be 626. In the 310 area, the new code will be 562, and will affect the areas from Long Beach and south. Both should be instituted in early 1997.

Directory assistance is 411, and repair service is 611. For the correct time, dial 853- and any four digits.

Pacific Bell

Areas not serviced by GTE are serviced by Pacific Bell. To apply for new service, call 800-559-2355. Assuming you have a credit history with a telephone company, you will not be required to pay a deposit if you have not had your service temporarily or completely disconnected in the last year for non-payment, and you have paid all previous "final" bills older than 45 days. In addition, a one-time charge to install your service may vary, depending on the type of work that is done. Pacific Bell offers all kinds of extra services for fees, including voice mail, call waiting, call blocking, repeat dialing, and number referral services. For a complete list of the services available, check the front White Pages Section of the *Pacific Bell Yellow Pages*, or ask your customer service representative for a brochure.

If you have billing questions, you should call 800-559-8899.

Long-Distance Telephone Carriers

At the time you install your telephone service, you will be asked to name a long-distance carrier. Most long-distance carriers now bill through your local carrier, so you get one telephone bill, rather than two. The largest carriers are **AT&T** (800-222-0300), **MCI** (800-888-8000), and **US Sprint** (800-877-7746).

Renter's Insurance

Once you have settled in, take a look around your apartment. Try to assess how much it would cost to replace the items you own at home: your stereo, television, wardrobe, furniture, etc. Amazing how it adds up, isn't it? By now you may be convinced of the need for renter's insurance. Policies vary, but renter's insurance can protect you from theft, fire damage, and the like. In some cases, you can get extra coverage to insure the contents of your home from damage due to earthquakes.

You can purchase renter's insurance through most insurance companies. As with all insurance, be sure you understand your policy completely, and ask questions.

Television Stations

Heaven forbid you should miss an episode of your favorite TV show! Here is where you can find the major television network affiliates in Los

Angeles. Channel 2 is **CBS,** Channel 4 is **NBC,** Channel 7 is **ABC,** Channel 11 is **Fox,** and Channel 28 is **PBS.** The large local stations are Channel 5 **KTLA,** Channel 9 **KCAL,** and Channel 13 **KCOP.** Check the daily Calendar section in the *Los Angeles Times* for a detailed list of television programming.

Cable Television

Aside from the ability of getting a zillion stations, cable also offers better reception in some areas. There are two main cable companies that service the Los Angeles area; they are **Century Cable** (310-828-2111) and **Continental Cable** (310-649-5050). The monthly fee for basic cable is approximately $25 - $33.

Department of Motor Vehicles (DMV)

New residents who come from out of state need to register vehicles in California within 20 days. Take your most recently issued registration, smog certificate and purchase information to your nearest **DMV** office.

In addition, California residents who drive motor vehicles on public highways must have a valid California driver's license. When you make your home in the state, you must apply for a California driver's license within 10 days. If you don't drive, but need a valid identification, the DMV is the place to go as well.

Unfortunately, DMV's are notorious for their long lines. In some instances, you can make an appointment, so do try. Following are the DMV offices in the Los Angeles area:

Culver City, 11400 West Washington Boulevard
Information: 310-271-4585
Appointments: 310-390-4026

Hollywood, 803 North Cole Avenue
Information: 213-744-2000
Appointments: 213-736-3101

Inglewood, 621 North La Brea Avenue
Information: 213-744-2000
Appointments: 213-412-6186

Santa Monica, 2235 Colorado Avenue
Information: 310-271-4585
Appointments: 310-453-5513

Parking

Parking regulations vary from neighborhood to neighborhood. Some areas require residents to display a parking permit to park on the street in front of their apartment building. Many areas that are close to shopping and business districts allow only two hour parking, unless your permit shows you to be a local resident. Some parts of Beverly Hills allow no overnight parking on the street.

The best advice is to read carefully the signs in your neighborhood. If permits are required for on-street parking, contact the permit department in your local city hall.

Stolen Cars

As a preventive measure, some local police departments (San Fernando Valley and Westside, for instance) allow you to register your car with them, giving them free reign to pull your car over if they see it being driven late at night or very early in the morning, when most thefts take place. By putting a yellow sticker on the rear window, owners signal that they will allow police to stop their cars without cause between the hours of 1 and 5 a.m. So far, the program has been a successful theft deterrent.

If your car has been stolen, contact the police department as soon as possible. Once you file a report, the police department will notify you as soon as your car has been located. If you have engraved your license number on your tape deck, car phone, and other accessories, the police can better identify those items should they be recovered.

Voter Registration

The Los Angeles County Registrar of Voters can be reached at 213-721-1100. For absentee ballots, call 213-725-5752. **The State of California Voters' Hot Line** is 800-345-8683.

Passports

You can apply for a passport at the **Federal Building,** 11000 Wilshire Boulevard, Room 13100, Westwood. For passport information, call 310-575-7070. Office hours are from 9 a.m. - 4 p.m. Many passport renewals can be handled by mail, so call ahead to check if you can avoid the long lines. You should allow three weeks between the time you turn in your application and the time you receive your passport.

You must apply in person if you are applying for the first time, if your most recent passport was applied for more than 12 years ago, or if your last passport was lost or stolen. In any of these cases, you will need to submit proof of U.S. citizenship, two identical photos taken within the last six months, evidence of identity, an application fee, and a completed passport application form, DSP-11. Passports are valid for 10 years.

Libraries

You can apply for a library card at any local library (check the "Neighborhoods" section at the beginning of this book for the one nearest you). Aside from the local city and county libraries, non-students can use the libraries at the many colleges and universities in the Los Angeles area. For more information, call the following public schools:

California State University Los Angeles, 213-343-3000
California State University Northridge, 818-885-1200
Los Angeles City College, 213-953-4000
Santa Monica College, 310-450-5150
University of California, Los Angeles 310-825-4321
West Los Angeles College, 310-287-4200

Recycling

Recycling is a way of life in Los Angeles. Some neighborhoods have curbside pickup, others have drop-off points. For information on recycling round-ups throughout Los Angeles County, call 800-552-5218. Residents of Malibu can arrange for home pick-up service by calling 310-457-7283. Santa Monica has a community recycling center plus curbside pick-up and centralized bins; for information call 310-458-8526.

T HE FOLLOWING services can further help you settle into your new home. Can't quite afford all the furniture you need? Need a hair trim? Have to find a place to store the chest of drawers that just won't fit in your bedroom? Here are some places to call.

Appliance Rental

Some apartments do not come with refrigerators and/or other appliances. **Wertz Brothers,** a family owned and operated business since 1931, can help. They sell and lease used appliances and furniture at these three locations:

Los Angeles, 210 North Western Avenue, 213-462-3155
San Fernando Valley, 14550 Victory Boulevard, 818-997-7951
West Los Angeles, 11879 Santa Monica Boulevard, 310-477-4251

Furniture Rental

If you're just getting settled and haven't had time to buy furniture yet, or perhaps you want some time to shop around for just the right pieces, here are some places where you can rent furniture, for both the office and home. Most places offer free pick-up and delivery, with purchase options.

• **Brooks,** five locations:
Beverly Hills, 8549 Wilshire Boulevard, 310-652-6795
Brentwood, 11843 Wilshire Boulevard, 310-479-4494
Los Angeles, 655 South Hope Street, 213-624-1202
Sherman Oaks, 15125 Ventura Boulevard, 818-386-2158
Manhattan Beach, 310-937-1519 (By appointment only)

- **Evans,** five locations:
  Beverly Hills, 8668 Wilshire Boulevard, 310-855-1148
  Los Angeles, 626 Wilshire Boulevard, 213-626-5773
  Marina del Rey, 4161 Lincoln Boulevard, 310-301-2577
  Sherman Oaks, 14140 Ventura Boulevard, 818-907-5496
  Westlake, 960-1 South Westlake Boulevard, 805-379-0007

Television and VCR Rental

Television and VCR rental companies often offer lease-to-buy options. Be sure to ask what their policy is on service; some offer it free of charge.

- **House Call**, Culver City, 310-397-1681
- **Norm's TV and Sound**, 11326 Idaho Avenue, West Los Angeles, 310-479-3726

Haircuts

Hair salons in Los Angeles run the gamut from Beverly Hills' high-priced chic ones (e.g. President Clinton's infamous $200 trim by Cristophe) to SuperCuts. Listed below are a very few of the hundreds of salons here; they represent a cross-section of what's available. When you look in the telephone directory under "Beauty Salons" you will be awed by the number you see listed.

SuperCuts, the nationwide chain, might be a good option for people who don't want to spend a fortune on a hair cut. The salons are essentially the same everywhere, and while you might not get a glass of white wine or a cappuccino while you wait, you can get a good basic style for about $9. The salons are located all over the city; just check the telephone directory or call information for the one nearest you.

Also, **The Vidal Sassoon Academy** offers inexpensive haircuts by their students. The cost is $15 Monday through Friday, and $20 on Saturday. The Academy is located at 1222 Third Street Promenade, Santa Monica, 310-393-1461.

Allen Edwards Salon offers the hip, LA haircut experience at relatively reasonable prices. Located at 3110 Main Street, Santa Monica (310-274-8575), most stylists charge $45 - $50 for a haircut, although Allen himself charges $75. Also located in Santa Monica, **Kenneth George Salon** cuts start at $45. They are located at 1914 Wilshire Boulevard, 310-453-5497.

A hot spot often mentioned in magazine articles touting the best salons is **Doyle Wilson,** at 8006 Melrose Avenue in Los Angeles (213-658-6987). Cuts here start at from $60-70.

And, for truly big spenders, you too can have your hair cut by stylist to President Clinton and the stars, Cristophe. Cuts by other stylists in the salon start at $75. To get Cristophe to trim your locks costs $250 the first time, and $200 thereafter. **Cristophe Salon** is located at 348 North Beverly Drive in where else, Beverly Hills (310-274-0851).

House Cleaning

For those who want the luxury of maid service, there are plenty of options. Check the telephone directory under "House Cleaning" for a complete listing of agencies near you, ask your landlord if she/he can recommend a good independent housekeeper, or try one of those listed below. If you choose a service, make sure it's bonded and insured. Also, since many house cleaning personnel in Los Angeles are Spanish-speaking, you may want to ask for someone with good English language skills, unless you speak a little Spanish or feel that you can make your needs known.

- **A Touch of Class,** 310-207-8503
- **Custom Maid,** 800-564-6484
- **Domesti-Care,** 310-459-9900
- **La Maison Agency,** 310-553-3509
- **Triple 9 Contractors,** 213-444-0027
- **Young's Maintenance Company,** 310-474-1234

Mail and Telephone

To have your telephone answered or to receive mail if you haven't yet found an apartment, you can contract with mail and telephone receiving companies. These services are also a good option for people frequently out of town. Aside from mailbox companies, mailboxes can also be rented at your local post office.

- **Mail Boxes Etc.** has several locations in Los Angeles, plus, they are open on Saturdays:
  Bel Air, 2337 Roscomare Road, #2, 310-440-9325
  Beverly Hills, 9016 Wilshire Boulevard, 310-274-7721
  Brentwood, 11718 Barrington Court, 310-472-8850
  Hollywood, 7095 Hollywood Boulevard, 213-850-5346
  Marina del Rey, 13428 Maxella Avenue, 310-827-4000
  Pacific Palisades, 15332 Antioch Street, 310-459-9739
  Santa Monica, 1223 Wilshire Boulevard, 310-458-6878
  West Hollywood, 7605 Santa Monica Boulevard, 213-656-7788
  West Hollywood, 8205 Santa Monica Boulevard, 213-656-4090

West Los Angeles, 11301 West Olympic Boulevard, 310-445-4014
West Los Angeles, 10573 West Pico Boulevard, 310-474-7383

Telephone answering services offer options such as call-forwarding, paging, wake-up calls, and voice mail, whatever suits your needs. For a complete listing, check the telephone directory under "Telephone Answering Service" or try one of these:

• **A-1 Answering Service,** 310-821-8855
• **American Message Center,** 213-872-0001
• **Post-Tel Business Center,** 310-828-8645
• **Professional Communications Network,** 800-627-4235
• **Shaumann Communications Services,** 310-473-7900

Storage

When you move into your new pad and find that there's just not enough room for all your belongings, you may need to put some things in storage. Following is a listing of a few of the many self-storage facilities in town. If you need professional help moving and storing your goods, check the telephone directory under "Movers & Full Service Storage".

• **E-Z Self Storage.** Call 800-488-8880 for location nearest you.
• **Mini Storage** has three West Los Angeles locations:
  Airport, 310-645-0900
  Culver City, 310-398-5000
  West Los Angeles, 310-398-5000
• **Public Storage** has more than 130 locations in Greater Los Angeles, call 800-447-8673 for the one nearest you.

S HOPPING is a favorite pastime in Los Angeles, and in recent years houseware and furniture stores have been cropping up all over town. Serious interior design shoppers might want to check out the Pacific Design Center and neighboring areas in West Hollywood (see "Neighborhoods" chapter), the interior design Mecca of the Los Angeles area. If prices are too high around there, at least it can give you some good ideas.

This guide begins with a list of full-service department stores where you can do a good portion of your shopping, then goes on to list specialty stores, where you can find more specific items.

Department Stores/Malls

Some residents think mall shopping is an indoor sport in Los Angeles.

Most of the full-service department stores like **Robinson's May** and **Macy's** can be found in the larger malls. Here are the major malls, and the big department stores that anchor them:

The Beverly Center, Beverly and La Cienega Boulevards, Los Angeles, 310-854-0070. This mall includes The Broadway and Macy's.
Century City Shopping Center, 10250 Santa Monica Boulevard, Century City, 310-277-3898. Macy's and Bloomingdale's are the two major department stores here.
Fox Hills Mall, Slauson and Sepulveda Boulevards, Culver City 310-397-3146. Major department stores include The Broadway, Robinson's May, and JC Penny.
Santa Monica Place, Third St. Promenade at Broadway, Santa Monica, 310-394-5451. Robinson's and Macy's anchor this mall.
Sherman Oaks Galleria, 15301 Ventura Boulevard, Sherman Oaks, 818-783-7100. Robinson's May and Robinson's are the major department stores here.

The Westside Pavilion, 10800 West Pico Boulevard, West Los Angeles, 310-474-6255. Major department stores include Nordstrom and Robinson's May.

For the area's chicest department stores, head to where else, Beverly Hills. Along Wilshire Boulevard is **Neiman-Marcus, Sak's Fifth Avenue,** and **Barney's,** and a **Bloomingdale's** is being constructed on North Beverly Drive.

Cameras & Electronics & Appliances

- **Adray's Discount Department Stores**
  Canoga Park, 8349 Topanga Canyon Boulevard, 818-348-2600
  Lakewood, 5615 Woodruff Avenue, 310-975-8722
  Los Angeles, 5575 Wilshire Boulevard, 213-935-8191
  Torrance, 4142 Pacific Coast Highway, 310-378-6777
  Van Nuys, 6609 Van Nuys Boulevard, 818-908-1500
  West Los Angeles, 11201 West Pico Boulevard, 310-479-0797
- **Circuit City,** 3115 South Sepulveda Boulevard, Los Angeles, 310-391-3144
- **The Good Guys**
  Los Angeles, 100 North La Cienega Boulevard, 310-659-6500
  Marina del Rey, 13450 Maxella Avenue, 310-574-1810
  West Los Angeles, 10831 West Pico Boulevard, 310-441-4600

Carpets and Rugs

- **Carpeteria**
  Hollywood, 1122 North Vine Street, 213-462-6232
  Santa Monica, 614 Santa Monica Boulevard, 310-394-0228
  Torrance, 4236 Artesia Boulevard, 310-542-6696
  West Los Angeles, 10670 West Pico Boulevard, 310-838-3181
- **IKEA,** 600 North San Fernando Boulevard, Burbank, 818-842-4532
- **Pier 1 Imports** (locations throughout the city, check your telephone directory)

Computers

- **1st Computer,** 1740 Westwood Boulevard, West Los Angeles, 310-478-2501
- **Connecting Point,** three locations:
  Los Angeles, 362 South La Brea Boulevard, 213-857-0371
  Pasadena, 277 South Lake Street, 818-584-1111

San Fernando Valley, 23647 Calabasas Road, 818-222-3822
- **LA Computer Center,** 12002 Pico Boulevard, West Los Angeles, 310-479-0999
- **ASUCLA Computer Store,** 308 Westwood Plaza, Westwood, 310-825-6952
For Macintosh sales, leasing, and service:
- **Personal Support,** 10431 Santa Monica Boulevard, West Los Angeles, 310-474-1633

Furniture

There is a proliferation of large, trendy, affordable furniture stores in the Los Angeles area. Here are some of the biggies:

- **Blueprint,** 8366 Beverly Boulevard, Los Angeles, 213-653-2439
- **Civilization,** 8884 Venice Boulevard, Los Angeles, 310-202-8883
- **Horizon,** 8600 West Pico Boulevard, Los Angeles, 213-655-8800
- **IKEA,** 600 North San Fernando Boulevard, Burbank, 818-842-4532
- **Pier 1 Imports** (locations throughout the city, check your telephone directory)
- **Plummer's,** 8876 Venice Boulevard, Los Angeles, 310-837-0138
- **Z Gallerie,** (locations throughout the city, check your telephone directory)

Grocery Stores

The big chain markets in Los Angeles are **Ralph's, Von's,** and the more upscale versions of Von's, **Pavilions Place.** Here are a few other options:

- **Erewhon Natural Food Market,** 7660 Beverly Blvd., Los Angeles, 213-937-0777. This is a health food store with a busy juice bar/deli.
- **Gelson's,** Century City Mall, 10250 Santa Monica Boulevard, 310-277-4288. Gelson's is big, beautiful, and pricey.
- **Trader Joe's** has more than fifty location on the West Coast, and is known for its specialty foods and wine sections.
  Culver City, 10011 Washington Boulevard, 310-202-1108
  Manhattan Beach, 1821 Manhattan Beach Boulevard, 310-372-1274
  Silver Lake 7238 Hyperion Avenue, 213-665-6774
  West Los Angeles, 10840 National Boulevard, 310-470-1917.
  West Hollywood 7304 Santa Monica, 213-851-9772
- **Mrs. Gooch's** pretty, natural food stores have three locations:
  Beverly Hills, 239 North Crescent Drive, 310-274-3360
  Redondo Beach, 405 North Pacific Coast Highway, 310-376-6931
  West Los Angeles, 3476 Centinela Avenue, 310-391-5209

• **Wild Oats,** 1425 Montana Avenue, Santa Monica, 310-576-4707.
Includes a popular juice bar.

Farmers' Markets

There are numerous popular farmers' markets throughout the city, including the famous, permanent **Farmers' Market at Third and Fairfax,** which features not only produce but food stalls, butchers, and tourist-oriented shops, as well. Below are some of the many neighborhood outdoor farmers markets that sell fruits, eggs, fish, vegetables, honey, nuts, cut flowers, plants, and more. Many stalls feature organically grown produce, but be sure to ask, or look for the certified organic sign, if that's important to you.

Beverly Hills
• 300 block of North Canon Drive, Sundays 9 a.m. -1 p.m.,
310-285-1048
Burbank
• 3rd Street and Palm Avenue, Saturdays 8 a.m. - 2 p.m.
Culver City
• Culver and Main parking lot, Tuesdays 3 - 7 p.m., 310-287-3850
Hollywood
• Ivar Avenue and Hollywood Boulevard, Sundays 8:30 a.m. - 1 p.m.
213-936-8143
Los Angeles
• 8th Street and Westmoreland Avenue, Mondays 1:30 - 4:30 p.m.
• Adams Boulevard and Vermont Avenue, Agnes Catholic Church
parking lot, Wednesdays 1 - 5 p.m. during the Summer, 2 - 5 p.m.
remainder of the year
Pasadena
• Villa Park Neighborhood Center, Tuesdays 9:30 a.m. - 1:30 p.m.
• City Hall, Allendale Branch Library, Thursdays 4 - 7 p.m.
• Victory, Pasadena High School parking lot, Saturdays 9 a.m. - 1 p.m.
Santa Monica
• Arizona Avenue and 2nd Street, Wednesdays 9:30 a.m. - 3 p.m.,
Saturdays 8:30 a.m. - 12 p.m., 310-458-8712
• Pico Boulevard and Cloverfield Avenue, Saturdays 9 a.m. - 1 p.m.
310-58-8712
• 2640 Main Street, Sundays 10 a.m. - 2 p.m., 310-458-8712
Venice
• Venice and Ocean Boulevards, Friday 7 - 11 a.m., 310-399-6690
West Hollywood
• Santa Monica Boulevard and Vista Street, Plummers Park,
Mondays 9 a.m. - 2 p.m., 310-967-4202

Hardware, Paints and Wallpaper

- **Armstrong's,** 8985 Venice Boulevard, Los Angeles, 310-477-8023
- **B & B,** 12450 West Washington Boulevard, Los Angeles, 310-390-9413
- **HomeBase,** 12727 Sherman Way, North Hollywood, 818-503-9082
- **Koontz,** 8914 Santa Monica Boulevard, West Hollywood, 310-652-0123

Kitchenware

- **Bed Bath & Beyond,** 11801 West Olympic Boulevard, West Los Angeles, 310-478-5767
- **Crate & Barrel,** Century City Mall, 10250 Santa Monica Boulevard, 310-551-1100
- **Pottery Barn** is in the Beverly Center (310-657-7505), Century City Mall (310-552-0170), and Santa Monica Place (310-393-1471). Check the beginning of this chapter for addresses.
- **Williams Sonoma** is in the Beverly Center (310-652-9117) and Santa Monica Place (310-451-7633). Check the beginning of this chapter for addresses. There is also a store in Beverly Hills at 317 North Beverly Drive, 310-274-9127.

Lamps and Lighting

- **IKEA,** 600 North San Fernando Boulevard, Burbank, 818-842-4532
- **Lamps Plus,** 2012 South Bundy Drive, West Los Angeles, 310-820-7567

Second-hand Shopping

A popular and inexpensive way to shop for clothes and jewelry is in second-hand stores. Merchandise runs the gamut from trendy to tacky to vintage. Check your telephone directory under "Clothing - Used" for listings in your area, or try one of the following spots:

- **All American Hero,** 314 Santa Monica Boulevard, Santa Monica, 310-395-4452
- **American Rag,** 150 South La Brea Boulevard, Los Angeles, 213-935-3154
- **Polkadots and Moonbeams,** 8367 West Third, Fairfax District, 213-651-1746

- **Supply Sergeant:**
  1431 Lincoln Boulevard, Santa Monica, 310-458-4166
  6664 Hollywood Boulevard, Hollywood, 213-463-4730
- **The Wasteland,** 7428 Melrose Avenue, West Hollywood, 213-653-3028
- For second-hand furniture, try one of the following **Wertz Brothers** locations:
  Los Angeles, 210 North Western Avenue, 213-462-3155
  San Fernando Valley, 14550 Victory Boulevard, 818-997-7951
  West Los Angeles, 11879 Santa Monica Boulevard, 310-477-4251

Also, the **Rose Bowl Swap Meet** is one of the largest flea markets in the Los Angeles area. It is held the second Sunday of every month from 9 a.m. – 3 p.m., and the cost is $5. Some of the hip Los Angeles furniture retailers shop here, and after some touch-up work on their swap meet purchases, resell them in their stores. Another smart source for used goods is *The Recycler,* a newspaper that comes out each Thursday and is available at most liquor stores.

Sporting Goods

- **Adventure 16** features equipment for camping and backpacking in:
  Tarzana, 5425 Reseda Boulevard, 818-345-4266
  West Los Angeles, 11161 West Pico Boulevard, 310-473-4574
- **Big Five,** 6601 Wilshire Boulevard, Los Angeles, 213-651-2909
- **Oshman's,**
  11110 West Pico Boulevard, West Los Angeles, 310-478-0446
  10800 West Pico Boulevard, West Los Angeles, 310-474-2321
- **Sport Chalet,** 100 North La Cienega Boulevard, Los Angeles, 310-657-3210

Towels and Linens

- **Bed, Bath & Beyond:**
  11801 West Olympic Boulevard, West Los Angeles, 310-478-5767
  Beverly Center, La Cienega and Beverly Boulevards, 310-652-1380
- **Strouds:**
  Los Angeles, 100 North La Cienega Boulevard, 310-657-2422
  Santa Monica, 3006 Wilshire Boulevard, 310-828-4455
  Westwood, 10830 Santa Monica Boulevard, 310-470-7606
  For bargains try **Strouds Clearance Center,**
  8104 Beverly Boulevard, Fairfax District, 213-655-5780

L IKE MOST major U.S. cities, finding good day care can be a problem, and waiting lists abound for the places with good reputations. The snootiest services even take waiting lists for unborn children, so be forewarned. The following organizations offer resources and referrals for day care, and cover everything from high-end to financially assisted options. You can get information and referrals to licensed child care providers, Head Start programs, and subsidized day care.

- **Child and Family Services,** Echo Park, 213-472-2700
- **Child Care Information Service,** Arcadia, 818-445-3311
- **Child Care Resource Center,** North Hollywood, 818-762-0905
- **Children's Home Society,** Long Beach, 310-901-3145
- **Connections for Children,** Santa Monica, 310-452-3202
- **Crystal Stairs,** Los Angeles, 213-299-0199
- **Mexican-American Opportunity Foundation,** Montebello, 213-890-9616
- **Options: A Child Care and Human Services Agency,** Baldwin Park, 818-856-5900

Nanny agencies are listed in your *Yellow Pages* under "Baby Sitters". It is common for in-home child care workers in Los Angeles to be from Spanish-speaking countries, so be sure to check on the English fluency of workers if your Spanish skills are not good enough to communicate your needs, or if you prefer an English-speaker assisting with your children.

Baby-sitting

The best source for baby-sitting is to ask around. If you belong to a church or synagogue, that can be a good source for referrals. Also, you might want to ask for referrals from neighbors or co-workers with children. Regardless of whom you find to baby-sit, it's always a good idea to ask for references.

THE LOS ANGELES area offers places of worship for a wide variety of religious preferences. While LA is not known as a town of one particular religion (for example, Boston is known as a Catholic center), here there is a large Protestant community, a large Roman Catholic community (due in part to the fact that LA has the largest Latino population in the United States), and the second largest Jewish population in the United States, behind the New York metropolitan area.

What follows is a sampling of the places of worship available. A quick look in the telephone directory should provide you with all of the religious centers in your neighborhood.

African Methodist Episcopal

First AME Church, Los Angeles, 213-730-9180
First AME Church, 1700 North Raymond Avenue, Pasadena, 818-798-0503

Armenian

Armenian Brotherhood Bible Church, 1536 East Washington Boulevard, Pasadena, 818-791-7773
Armenian Church of the Nazarene, 1480 East Washington Boulevard, Pasadena, 818-398-8108

Assembly of God

Assembly of God First, 1320 Arizona Avenue, Santa Monica, 310-393-5763
Faith Tabernacle, Purdue and Olympic Boulevard, West Los Angeles, 310-473-3135

New Life Assembly of God, 330 North Hill Avenue, Pasadena, 818-795-8592

Baha'i

Baha'i Faith Los Angeles Center, 5755 Rodeo Road, Los Angeles, 213-933-8291

Baptist

Community Baptist Church, 1234 Artesia Boulevard, Manhattan Beach, 310-372-3516
First Baptist Church of Pasadena, 75 North Marengo Avenue, Pasadena, 818-793-7164
First Baptist Church of West Los Angeles, 1609 South Barrington Avenue, West Los Angeles, 310-826-8374
New Mount Calvary Missionary Baptist Church, 402 East El Segundo Boulevard, El Segundo, 310-324-0644

Buddhist

Soka Gakkai International, 1212 7th Street, Santa Monica, 310-451-4422
West Los Angeles Buddhist Church, 2003 Corinth, West Los Angeles, 310-477-7274

Christian Science

Christian Science Churches and Organizations, 1133 South Bundy Drive, West Los Angeles, 310-820-2014
First Church of Christ Scientist, 1401 North Crescent Heights Boulevard, West Hollywood, 213-656-2888
First Church, 550 East Green Street, Pasadena, 818-793-5151
Third Church, 2803 East Colorado Boulevard, Pasadena, 818-793-7345

Eastern Orthodox

Saint Mark Coptic Orthodox Church, 1600 South Robertson Boulevard, Los Angeles, 310-275-3050

Episcopal

All Saints Episcopal Church, 132 North Euclid Avenue, Pasadena,
818-796-1172
Saint Mary's Episcopal Church, 3647 Watseka Avenue, Los Angeles,
310-558-3834
Saint Michael's Episcopal Church, 361 Richmond Avenue,
El Segundo, 310-322-2589

Islam

Islamic Studies and Recruitment Center, 14534 Arminta, Van Nuys,
818-787-0911
Masjid Bilal, 4016 South Central Avenue, Los Angeles, 213-233-7274

Jehovah's Witness

Jehovah's Witness, 608 East Grand Avenue, El Segundo,
310-322-0788
Jehovah's Witness, 2119 Virginia Avenue, Santa Monica,
310-452-3825
Jehovah's Witness East, 3493 East Del Mar Boulevard, Pasadena,
818-449-4890

Jewish - Conservative

Beth Am, 1039 South La Cienega Boulevard, Los Angeles,
213-655-6401
Kehillat Ma'arav, 1715 21st Street, Santa Monica, 310-829-0566
Mishkon Tephilo, 206 Main Street, Venice, 310-392-3029
Sephardic Temple Tifereth Israel, 10500 Wilshire Boulevard, West Los
Angeles, 310-475-7311
Sinai Temple, 10400 Wilshire Boulevard, West Los Angeles,
310-474-1518

Jewish - Orthodox

Beth Jacob, 9030 West Olympic Boulevard, Beverly Hills,
310-278-1911
Chabad, 1111 Montana Avenue, Santa Monica, 310-394-5699
Pacific Jewish Center, 505 Ocean Front Walk, Venice, 310-392-8749

Jewish - Reconstructionist

Kehillath Israel, 16019 Sunset Boulevard, Pacific Palisades, 310-459-2328

Jewish - Reform

Beth Shir Shalom, 1827 California Street, Santa Monica, 310-453-3361
Leo Baeck Temple, 1300 Sepulveda Boulevard, Bel Air, 310-476-2861
Stephen S. Wise Temple, 15500 Stephen S. Wise Drive, Bel Air, 310-476-8561
Temple Isaiah, 10345 West Pico Boulevard, West Los Angeles, 310-277-2772
University Synagogue, 11960 Sunset Boulevard, West Los Angeles, 310-472-1255
Wilshire Boulevard Temple, 3663 Wilshire Boulevard, Los Angeles, 213-388-2401

Lutheran

Grace Lutheran Church, 4427 Overland Avenue, Culver City, 310-559-1027
First Lutheran Church, 808 North Los Robles Avenue, Pasadena, 818-793-1139
First Lutheran Church, 1100 Poinsettia Avenue, Manhattan Beach, 310-545-5653
St. John's Lutheran Church, 1611 East Sycamore Avenue, El Segundo, 310-615-1072

Methodist

Crescent Heights United Methodist Church of West Hollywood, 1296 North Fairfax Avenue, West Hollywood, 213-656-5336
Culver-Palms United Methodist Church, 4464 Sepulveda Boulevard, Culver City, 310-390-7717
Holliston United Methodist Church, 1305 East Colorado Boulevard, Pasadena, 818-793-0685
United Methodist Church, 540 Main Street, El Segundo, 310-322-0051
Westwood United Methodist Church, 10497 Wilshire Boulevard, Westwood, 310-474-4511

Mormon

The Church of Jesus Christ of Latter-Day Saints, 10777 Santa Monica Boulevard, Westwood, 310-474-1549
Jesus Christ of Latter Day Saints, 1215 E. Mariposa, El Segundo, 310-322-5370

Presbyterian

Bel Air Presbyterian Church, 16221 Mulholland Drive, Bel Air, 818-788-4200
Beverly Hills Presbyterian Church, 505 North Rodeo Drive, Beverly Hills, 310-271-5194
Brentwood Presbyterian Church, 12000 San Vicente Boulevard, Brentwood, 310-826-5656
Culver City Presbyterian Church, 11269 Washington Boulevard, Culver City, 310-398-3071
Pasadena Presbyterian Church, 54 North Oakland, Pasadena, 818-793-2191
West Hollywood Presbyterian Church, 7350 Sunset Boulevard, West Hollywood, 213-874-6646
Westwood Presbyterian Church, 10822 Wilshire Boulevard, Westwood, 310-474-4535

Protestant

Advent Christian
Iglesia Nueva Vida, 400 North Marengo Avenue, Pasadena, 818-795-8612

Roman Catholic

American Martyrs Catholic Church, 624 15th Street, Manhattan Beach, 310-545-5651
Good Shepherd, 505 North Bedford Drive, Beverly Hills, 310-276-3139
Saint Andrews, 311 North Raymond Avenue, Pasadena, 818-792-4183
Saint Monica's, 725 California Street, Santa Monica, 310-393-9287
Saint Philip, 151 South Hill Avenue, Pasadena, 818-793-0693
Saint Victor Church, 8634 Holloway Drive, West Hollywood, 310-652-6477

Science of Mind

Hollywood Church of Religious Science, 7677 Sunset Boulevard, Hollywood, 213-876-2260

PERHAPS because Los Angeles is the home of the entertainment industry, there are an infinite number of things to do here to occupy your leisure time. Whatever your interests, from music to theater to visual art, Los Angeles offers not only a wide variety from which you can choose, but some of the finest in the world.

If you want to find out what's going on this week or this month, here are a few publications to check out:

- The **LA Weekly** is the largest and most well-read free weekly newspaper in Los Angeles. Editorial coverage includes social and political issues, as well as extensive film, art, music and restaurant criticism. Each week, the Calendar section lists some fifty pages of events—everything from coffeehouse folk performances to Latin dance clubs to political symposiums. (Plus, the personal ads offer entertainment unto themselves!)
- The **LA Reader** is a free weekly that comes out every Thursday and also includes entertainment listings.
- The **LA Village View** is a third option, with similar coverage.
- The **Los Angeles Times** publishes a daily Calendar section listing show openings, plus a detailed Calendar section on Sunday.
- **Los Angeles,** a monthly city magazine, publishes entertainment listings in the back of the magazine.
- **Buzz,** the challenger to *Los Angeles*, also publishes an entertainment guide.

In addition, the **City of Los Angeles Cultural Affairs Department** sponsors a 24-hour, seven-days-a-week hot line with the latest information about music, art, dance, theater, special events, and festivals going on throughout Los Angeles. The telephone number is 213-688-ARTS.

Tickets to many events can be purchased through **Ticketmaster,** 213-480-3232.

Food

Philly has its cheesesteaks, and Chicago has its pizza. Well, if you ask a Los Angeleno about Los Angeles' equivalent fast food fame, they'll rave to you about **LA chili-cheeseburgers.** Perhaps it's the blend of Latino culture's chili with Americana's good old hamburger; whatever the reason, the chili-cheeseburgers here are famous to locals, and everyone swears by their favorite burger joint. A close second in popularity to the chili-cheeseburger is either hot-dogs or tacos.

While it would be presumptuous and difficult to name the city's finest restaurants, here are some of the places that junk-food junkies call heaven:

- **The Apple Pan,** 10801 Pico Boulevard, Westwood, 310-475-3585. This Westwood institution is known for its burgers, and for its pies.
- **Carney's,** 8351 West Sunset Boulevard, West Hollywood, 213-654-8300. Housed in an old train car, Carney's aficionados swear by the chili-burgers and chili-fries.
- **Fatburger,** various locations citywide. These spots stay open late, for those midnight cravings.
- **In-N-Out Burger,** various locations citywide. For the one nearest you, call 800-786-1000.
- **Marty's Hamburger Stand,** 10558 West Pico Boulevard, West Los Angeles, 310-836-6944. This is the original Marty's.
- **Marty's Hamburger Stand,** 1255 La Cienega Boulevard, Los Angeles, 310-652-8047. The brave here go for "The Combo", a chili-cheeseburger with a sliced hot-dog on top.
- **Pink's,** 709 North La Brea Boulevard, Los Angeles 213-931-4223. Open till 2 a.m. during the week and 3 a.m. on weekends, Pink's is a favorite late night chili-dog stop.
- **Tail o' the Pup,** 329 North San Vicente, West Hollywood, 652-4517. This spot is famous for its architecture; the stand is in the shape of a hot-dog.
- **Tito's Tacos,** 11222 Washington Place, Culver City, 310-391-5780. Don't be daunted by the line out front, it moves fast.
- **Tommy's,** various locations citywide. A popular burger joint with imitators all over the city.

Higher Education

Local colleges and universities offer many cultural and educational opportunities, from extension classes to concerts to lecture series. Following is a listing of some of the institutions of higher learning in the Los Angeles area:

- **Art Center College of Design,** 1700 Lida Street, Pasadena, 818-396-2200. Art Center is a four-year college known for its classes in both fine and applied arts.
- **California Institute of Technology,** 1201 East California Boulevard, Pasadena, 818- 395-6811. Cal Tech is a highly regarded school of science and mathematics, and the place where news cameras turn for information after local earthquakes.
- **California Institute of the Arts,** 24700 West McBean Parkway, Valencia, 805-255-1050. This avant-garde school known as Cal Arts focuses on visual, theatrical, and written arts.
- **Loyola Marymount University,** 7101 West 80th Street, Westchester, 310-338-2700. This private four-year school (with graduate programs, as well) is located near the Los Angeles airport.
- **•Los Angeles City College,** 855 North Vermont Avenue, Los Angeles, 213-953-4000. This is a large, two-year community college with an ethnically mixed student body and an urban environment.
- **Mount Saint Mary's College,** 12001 Chalon Road, West Los Angeles, 310-476-2237. Located in the scenic hills above Brentwood with views of the city below, this Catholic school holds art gallery shows and other cultural events.
- **Pasadena City College,** 1570 E Colorado Boulevard, Pasadena, 818-585-7123. This two-year community college hosts cultural events, as well as special programs for part-time students.
- **Pepperdine University,** 24255 West Pacific Coast Highway, Malibu, 310-456-4000. Who can concentrate at this private school with such a magnificent ocean view?
- **Santa Monica College,** 1900 Pico Boulevard, Santa Monica, 310-450-5150. SMC is a well-respected, two-year community college with a high transfer rate to UCLA.
- **•University of California, Los Angeles,** 405 Hilgard Avenue, Westwood, 310-825-4321. UCLA has the largest enrollment of all nine campuses in the UC system, with more than 35, 000 students. Walking tours of the pretty, 419-acre campus are available. Don't miss the Franklin D. Murphy Sculpture Garden.
- **University of Southern California,** Exposition Boulevard between Vermont Avenue and Figueroa Street, 213-740-2311. This private school has a number of galleries and museums open to the public, as well as displays of scripts and movie memorabilia at the Cinema Special Collections Library.

Comedy

Famous comedians often show up at various clubs around LA to try out new material, so you never know when you might be in for a special treat. There are several popular comedy clubs in and around Los Angeles, including the following:

- **Acme Comedy Theater,** 135 North La Brea Boulevard, Los Angeles, 213-525-0202
- **Comedy Store,** 8433 Sunset Boulevard, West Hollywood, 213-656-6225
- **Comedy Store West,** 1000 1/2 Gayley Avenue, Westwood, 310-208-0623
- **Groundlings Theatre,** 7307 Melrose Avenue, Los Angeles, 213- 934-9700. This improvisational comedy troupe was the training ground for several Saturday Night Live veterans, such as Phil Hartman and Julia Sweeney.
- **Ice House,** 24 North Mentor Avenue, Pasadena, 818-577-1894
- **Igby's,** 11637 West Pico Boulevard, West Los Angeles, 310-477-3553
- **Improvisation,** 8162 Melrose Avenue, Los Angeles, 213-651-2583
- **Laugh Factory,** 8001 Sunset Boulevard, Hollywood, 213-656-1336
- **MICE,** West Hollywood Playhouse, 666 North Robertson Boulevard, West Hollywood, 818-762-7547
- **Upfront Comedy Club,** 123 Broadway, Santa Monica, 310-319-3477. This club was formed by some former members of Second City.

Movie Theaters

Movies are very popular in Los Angeles. As the home of the film business, most films open here and in New York ahead of the rest of the country. In addition, you may be approached in front of theaters to attend market survey screenings, where you can watch a free movie in exchange for filling out a questionnaire at the end of the show. While the large multi-screen theaters are everywhere (the biggies are AMC, Mann, Pacific, General, and Edwards; check the telephone directory or newspaper for the one nearest you), here are a few **alternative theaters** that feature foreign, classic, budget and/or art films.

- **Aero,** Montana Avenue, Santa Monica, 310-395-4990. The Aero offers $5 double features of movies that have been out for a few months.
- **Laemmle Theatres**
  Beverly Hills: Music Hall, 9036 Wilshire Boulevard, 310-274-6869
  Encino: Town Center 5, 17200 Ventura Boulevard, 818-981-9811
  Pasadena: Esquire, 2670 East Colorado Boulevard, 818-793-6149;
  Colorado, 2588 East Colorado Boulevard, 818-796-9704
  Santa Monica: Monica, 1332 2nd Street, 310-394-9741
  West Hollywood: Sunset 5, 8000 Sunset Boulevard, 213-848-3500
  West Los Angeles: Royal, 11523 Santa Monica Boulevard, 310-477-5581

• **Landmark Theaters**
Santa Monica: NuWilshire, 1314 Wilshire Boulevard, 310-394-8099
South Pasadena: Rialto, 1023 South Fair Oaks, 818-799-9567
West Los Angeles: Nuart, 11272 Santa Monica Boulevard,
310-478-6379
Samuel Goldwyn Pavilion Cinemas, Westside Pavilion,
310-475-0202
• **Silent Movie,** 611 North Fairfax, Fairfax District, 310-0653-2389.
This theater features only "pre-talkies".

Art Museums

There are myriad fine museums, featuring both art and other exhibits,
scattered about Los Angeles. If you're up for an intensive day of muse-
um-hopping, you might want to head for what is known as "Museum
Row," the area along Wilshire Boulevard running east from Fairfax. In
these few blocks are located the Los Angeles County Museum of Art,
Craft and Folk Art Museum, Petersen Automotive Museum, Museum of
Miniatures, and the Page Museum at the La Brea Tarpits. It could make
for quite an eclectic outing! Or, if like most people you prefer to take in
just one or two museums a day, check out of the following:

• **J. Paul Getty Museum,** 17985 West Pacific Coast Highway,
Malibu, 310-458-2003. The site alone, on the Malibu cliffs overlook-
ing the Pacific Ocean, is worth the visit. This impressive and vast
collection of antiquities, European paintings and sculptures, draw-
ings, decorative arts, and photographs is free to view, but because
parking is limited, parking reservations are required. There is also a
shuttle from nearby parking lots (no reservations needed), private
automobile and cab drop-offs, or you can arrive via RTD bus line
434; call the museum for more information. A new Getty Center is
currently under construction (see "Brentwood" section in the
"Neighborhoods" chapter). Admission is free.
• **Craft and Folk Art Museum,** 5814 Wilshire Boulevard, Fairfax
District, 213-937-5544. International and American folk art are featured in the museum's new digs. Admission is $4, $2 for students
and seniors, and free for children under twelve.
• **Armand Hammer Museum of Art,** 10899 Wilshire Boulevard,
Westwood, 310-443-7000. The permanent collection features more
than five centuries of West European art, at this museum run by
UCLA.
• **Huntington Library and Gardens,** 1151 Oxford Road, Pasadena,
818-405-2141. The Huntington features an extensive European art
collection, a scholarly library, plus notable botanical gardens.
Suggested donation is $7.50 adults, $6 for seniors, and $4 for chil-
dren over twelve.

- **Los Angeles County Museum of Art (LACMA),** 5905 Wilshire Boulevard, Fairfax District, 213-857-6000. This extensive museum features everything from American and European art to photography to Indian and Southeast Asian art, plus a fine film department featuring lectures and screenings. If a major traveling exhibition is coming to Los Angeles, it will usually mount the show at LACMA. (For information on free musical performances held at LACMA, see the section entitled "Music" in this chapter.) Admission is $6 for adults, $4 for students and seniors, $1 for children aged six-seventeen, and free for children under six.
- **Museum of African-American Art,** 4005 South Crenshaw Boulevard, Third Floor, Los Angeles, 213-294-7071. Permanent and rotating exhibitions by African American artists, as well as seasonal events like an annual tree lighting ceremony at Christmas. Admission is free.
- **Museum of Contemporary Art (MOCA)** and 250 South Grand Avenue, Downtown, 213-626-6222. Permanent collection features painting, sculpture, live performances, and environmental work, all in a landmark building designed by Arata Isozaki. Free admission Thursdays from 5-8 p.m. General admission is $6, $4 for seniors and students, and children under twelve are admitted for free.
- **Norton Simon Museum of Art,** 411 West Colorado Boulevard, Pasadena, 818-449-6840. The permanent collection features European art from the Renaissance to the mid-20th century. Admission is $4 for adults, $2 for seniors and students.
- **Santa Monica Museum of Art,** 2437 Main Street, 310-399-0433. This small museum features changing contemporary exhibitions. An admission donation of $4 is recommended.
- **Skirball Museum,** 2701 North Sepulveda Boulevard, Brentwood, 310-440-4500. The Skirball features Jewish fine arts, archaeological artifacts, ceremonial and religious objects, photographs, and folk arts. This new location for the museum will open to the public in April of 1996.
- **The Temporary Contemporary,** 152 N. Central Avenue, Downtown, 213-626-6222. This museum began as a temporary space while MOCA was being built, but it continues now as an extra exhibit space for MOCA events.
- **Watts Towers,** 1727 East 107th Street, Watts, 213-847-4646. Though not a museum in the traditional sense, this monumental piece of folk art took artist Sam Rodia 33 years to complete. The towers are built of salvaged steel rods, dismantled pipes, bed frames and cement, and are covered with bottle fragments, ceramic tiles, china plates, and more than 70,000 seashells. The adjacent Watts Towers Art Center hosts visual and performing art exhibits, poetry readings and other events.

Museums

- **Autry Museum of Western Heritage,** 4700 Western Heritage Way, Griffith Park, 213-667-2000. In this museum founded by famed movie cowboy Gene Autry is a permanent collection features art and artifacts depicting the history of the American West. Admission is $7.50 for adults, $5 for seniors and students, and $3 for children two-twelve.
- **California Afro-American Museum,** South Figueroa Street and State Drive, Downtown, 213-744-7432. This museum focuses on African-American achievements in science, politics, religion, athletics, and the arts. Admission is free.
- **California Heritage Museum,** 2612 Main Street, Santa Monica, 310-392-8537. Admission is $2 (free for members and children under twelve) to view the rotating exhibits pertaining to California.
- **Fowler Museum of Cultural History,** UCLA, Westwood, 310-825-4361. Admission is free, but parking is $5 on the UCLA campus to visit this museum which features exhibits about cultural objects and art.
- **Griffith Park Observatory,** 2800 East Observatory Road, Griffith Park, 213-664-1191. There is free admission to the astronomy exhibits, and a charge of $3.50 for adults to get into the planetarium and laserium shows.
- **Hollywood Wax Museum,** 6767 Hollywood Boulevard, Hollywood, 213-462-5991. Admission is $8.95 for adults, $6.95 for children six-twelve.
- **Japanese-American National Museum,** 369 East First Street, Downtown, 213-625-0414. This cultural center illustrates the history of Japanese immigration to the United States. Admission is $4 for adults, $3 for seniors and students, and children under five are free.
- **The Carol & Barry Kaye Museum of Miniatures,** 5900 Wilshire Boulevard, Fairfax District, 213-937-6464. This permanent display of more than two hundred tiny fantasy worlds is located directly across the street from the Los Angeles County Museum of Art. Admission costs are $7.50 general, $6.50 for seniors, $5 for students twelve-eighteen, and $3 for children three-eleven.
- **Museum of Flying,** 2772 Donald Douglas Loop, Santa Monica, 310-392-8822. Features exhibits of flyable aircraft, which, on the weekends, take off. Admission is $7 for adults, $5 for seniors, $3 for children three-seventeen, and free for those under the age of three.
- **Museum of Jurassic Technology,** 941 Venice Boulevard, Palms, 310-836-6131. It's hard to characterize this place, except to say as they do that they feature "exhibits of idiosyncratic and curious things throughout the world." There is no admission fee, but a nominal donation is requested.

- **Museum of Natural History,** 900 Exposition Boulevard, Los Angeles, 213-744-3466. Free admission the first Tuesday of each month. Regular admission fees are $6 for adults, $3 for seniors and students, $2 for children five- twelve, and free for kids under five.
- **Museum of Science and Industry,** 700 State Drive, Los Angeles, 213-744-2034. Free to the public, except the changing large format films at the IMAX Theater.
- **Museum of Tolerance,** 9786 West Pico Boulevard, Beverly Hills, 310-553-9036. This facility features high-technology exhibits dedicated to the promotion of understanding among people of different races and religions. The foci are on the history of racism and prejudice in American history, and the Nazi Holocaust. Admission is $8 for adults, $6 for seniors over the age of sixty-two, $5 for students, and $3 for children aged three-eleven.
- **Page Museum at the La Brea Tarpits,** 5801 Wilshire Boulevard, Fairfax District, 213-857-6311. Features fossils from La Brea Tarpits, and other exhibits on paleontology. Admission is $6 for adults, $2 for children five-ten, and free for kids under five.
- **Petersen Automotive Museum,** 6060 Wilshire Boulevard, Fairfax District, 213-930-2277. Where else, besides perhaps Detroit, would you expect to find a museum devoted to our fascination with cars? Admission is $7 for adults, $5 for seniors and students, $3 for children five-twelve, and free for those under the age of five.
- **Southwest Museum,** 234 Museum Drive, Los Angeles, 213-221-2163. This is Los Angeles' first museum, founded in 1907, and it contains an important academic collection of Native American art and artifacts. Admission is $5 for adults, $3 for seniors or college students, $2 for children seven-eighteen, and free for those under the age of seven.

Music

For a complete listing of the week's musical offerings, check out the *LA Weekly,* which offers the most comprehensive guide to the vast LA music scene. What follows is an idea of what's available to suit your musical tastes.

Classical

Led by Esa-Pekka Salonen and recognized as one of the greatest orchestras in the world, the **LA Philharmonic Orchestra** presents a variety of concerts, recitals, and special programs at the Dorothy Chandler Pavilion in The Music Center and at the Hollywood Bowl. For information call **The Music Center,** 135 North Grand Avenue, Downtown, 213-972-7300.

The **Beverly Hills Symphony,** in existence since 1993 and led by conductor Bogidar Avramov, can be reached at 310-276-8385. Their summer series is held outdoors at Greystone Park on the grounds of the historic mansion there, and the winter series is held at various civic sites in Beverly Hills. And, the 50-year-old **Santa Monica Symphony Orchestra,** conducted by Allen Robert Gross, can be reached at 310-996-3260.

Choruses

- **Los Angeles Master Chorale,** 213-972-7282. This 120-voice symphonic chorus performs its subscription series at the Dorothy Chandler Pavilion at The Music Center.

Coffeehouse Performances

This relaxing venue for music, food, and socializing is very popular. Here are a few of the local coffeehouses that offer music and other performances on a regular basis, as well an alternative to the omnipresent Starbucks.

- **Anastasia's Asylum,** 1028 Wilshire Boulevard, Santa Monica, 310-394-7113
- **Congo Square,** 1238 Third Street Promenade, Santa Monica, 310-395-5606
- **Highland Grounds,** 742 North Highland Avenue, Hollywood, 213-466-1507
- **Insomnia,** 7286 Beverly Boulevard, Fairfax District, 213-931-4943
- **Insomnia Cafe,** 13718 Ventura Boulevard, Sherman Oaks, 818-990-9945. Believe it or not, this is a members only coffee house.
- **Kings Road Cafe,** 8361 Beverly Boulevard, Fairfax District, 213-655-9044
- **The Living Room,** 112 South La Brea Avenue, Fairfax District, 213-933-2933
- **Odeon,** 625 Montana Avenue, Santa Monica, 310-451-9096
- **Two Part,** 11769 Santa Monica Boulevard, West Los Angeles, 310-473-6135
- **Van Gogh's Ear,** 796 Main Street, Venice, 310-314-0022. Open 24 hours.

Country

- **The Cowboy Palace Saloon,** 21635 Devonshire Street, Chatsworth, 818-341-0166. Live country music and dancing seven nights a week.

- **Culver Saloon,** 11513 Washington Boulevard, Culver City, 310-391-1519. A country nightclub featuring local acts.
- **The Palomino,** 6907 Lankershim Boulevard, North Hollywood, 818-764-4018. This valley nightclub features country and more, in a laid-back setting. Cover charges to $15.

Dance

- **Golden West Ballet Theater,** 310-202-7005
- **Joffrey Ballet,** 213-487-8677
- **Los Angeles Classical Ballet,** 310-427-5206
- **Los Angeles Contemporary Dance Theater,** 213-932-8500
- **Los Angeles Modern Dance and Ballet,** 213-655-6812

Dance Clubs

Dance clubs come and go, in part due to the often unpredictable lives of local DJ's, promoters, and club owners. Some clubs exist at certain venues only on certain nights, or move around town each week or month. Your best bet is to consult the *LA Weekly's* listing of "Dance Clubs" in their "Calendar" section.

Jazz and R & B

- **Atlas Bar & Grill,** 3760 Wilshire Boulevard, Los Angeles, 213-380-8400. This Jazz club/restaurant is located inside the landmark Wiltern Theater.
- **Babe & Ricky's Inn,** 5259 South Central Avenue, Los Angeles, 213-235-4866. This is LA's longest running blues club, located on Central Avenue, which in the 50's was the heart of the city's African American music community.
- **The Baked Potato,** 3787 Cahuenga Boulevard, North Hollywood, 818-980-1615. A small, well-known jazz spot that serves 38 kinds of baked potatoes. Cover charge: $5 - $8.
- **The Baked Potato,** 26 East Colorado Boulevard, Pasadena, 818-564-1122. The second location.
- **B.B. King's Blues Club,** 1000 Universal Center Drive, Universal City, 818-6-BBKING. Sister to the flagship club in Memphis, this large dinner club features all kinds of live blues performances.
- **Catalina Bar & Grill,** 1640 North Cahuenga Boulevard, Los Angeles, 213-466-2210. Catalina is an upscale jazz supper club, often with big-name acts on the bill.
- **Harvelle's,** 1432 Fourth Street, Santa Monica, 310-395-1676. A funky, small blues spot that gets very crowded.

• **Jazz Bakery,** 3233 Helms Avenue, Culver City, 310-271-9039. The music-listeners place to hear local and touring jazz acts.
• **St. Mark's,** 23 Winward Avenue, Venice, 310-452-2222. This two-story dinner and music venue is situated just up the street from the Venice Boardwalk.

Latin, Brazilian and Spanish Clubs

• **El Floridita,** 1253 Vine Street, Hollywood, 213-871-8612. Cuban music and food.
• **Grand Avenue,** 1024 South Grand Avenue, Downtown, 213-747-0999. For all kinds of Latin dance sounds.
• **La Masia,** 9077 Santa Monica Boulevard, West Hollywood, 310-273-7066. A supper club featuring the cuisine of Northeastern Spain, plus live salsa and merengue music.
• **Zabumba,** 10717 Venice Boulevard, West Los Angeles, 310-841-6525. For Brazilian food, music, and fun.

Opera

World-class opera is performed from September through June in the **Dorothy Chandler Pavilion,** which is one of three performance spaces that make up The Music Center.

The Music Center is located at 135 North Grand Avenue, Downtown, 213-972-7211. Tickets may be purchased in person at The Music Center box office, or by calling **Ticketmaster,** 213-480-3232.

Reggae

• **Kingston 12,** 814 Broadway, Santa Monica, 310-451-4423. This is LA's only full-time reggae venue, though other clubs offer reggae on selected nights.

Rock and Pop

• **Al's Bar,** 305 South Newitt Street, Downtown, 213-625-9703. A gritty, trendy Downtown standard.
• **Alligator Lounge,** 3321 Pico Boulevard, Santa Monica, 310-449-1844. This Westside club is a popular place with the alternative music scene.
• **Coconut Teaszer,** 8121 Sunset Boulevard, Hollywood, 213-654-4887. Several bands play nightly, plus there's a space downstairs tor acoustic or eclectic performances.

- **14 Below,** 1348 14th Street, Santa Monica, 310-451-5040. Live music and dancing every night, plus pool, darts, and lots of beer on tap.
- **Molly Malone's Irish Pub,** 575 South Fairfax Avenue, Fairfax District, 213-935-2707. For Irish (and other) rock, folk, and R & B.
- **The Palace,** 1735 North Vine Street, Hollywood, 213-462-3000. A legendary club with a dance floor, balcony seating, and a patio.
- **Roxy Theatre,** 9009 Sunset Boulevard, West Hollywood, 310-276-2222. This venue often serves as a showcase for the music industry's newest signs. Cover charge: $8 - $15.
- **The Troubadour,** 9081 Santa Monica Boulevard, West Hollywood, 310-276-6168. A tried and true venue for live nightly live performances.
- **The Viper Room,** 8852 Sunset Boulevard, West Hollywood, 310-358-1880. This is the dark, smoky place now notorious as the site of River Phoenix's overdose. Cover charge: $3 - $6.
- **Whiskey-a-Go-Go,** 8901 Sunset Boulevard, West Hollywood, 310-652-4202. For years a popular rock-and-roll club, the Whiskey now features mostly heavy metal. Cover charge: $5 - $10.

For acoustic performances:

- **Genghis Cohen,** 740 North Fairfax Avenue, Fairfax District, 213-653-0640. This place is half Chinese restaurant, half music venue.
- **Luna Park,** 665 Robertson Boulevard, West Hollywood, 213-465-4762. This restaurant/music venue plays host to a variety of acts, from folk to Brazilian pop.
- **McCabe's Guitar Shop,** 3101 Pico Boulevard, Santa Monica, 310-828-4497. Yes it's a guitar store, but there's a back room that features fine acoustic performances. Cover charge: $10–$20.

Free Concerts

In addition to all of the above, there are often free concerts throughout the city, especially during the summer months. The city of Santa Monica sponsors a series of free summer concerts on Thursday nights from 7:30 - 9:30 p.m. on the Santa Monica Pier. Called the **Twilight Dance Series,** the featured musicians include jazz, rock, blues, salsa, gospel, and international artists. For more information, call 310-458-8900. The Century City Shopping Mall has a free outdoor jazz series called **Jazzopolis** on Wednesday evenings from 7:00 - 9:00 p.m. during the summer. For more information, call 310-277-3898. And, the **Los Angeles County Museum of Art** features a variety of free concerts, including live jazz in the museum's outdoor plaza every Friday night from 5:30 - 8:30 p.m., chamber music concerts in a museum auditorium on Sunday afternoons at 4:00 p.m., and Big Band concerts on selected Sunday afternoons throughout the summer. For more information, call 213-857-6000.

Television Tapings

If you would like to be an audience member at a live TV taping, write to the **Los Angeles Convention and Visitors Bureau,** #600, 633 West 5th Street, Los Angeles, CA 90017 and enclose a self-addressed, stamped envelope. Write to them well ahead of time, especially if you would like to see a popular show. They tend to be booked months in advance. A monthly calendar of television tapings is available when you send a self-addresses, stamped envelope to **Audiences Unlimited,** 100 Universal City Plaza, Building 153, Universal City, 91608. For a weekly listing, call 818-506-0067.

Theatre

There are dozens of fine productions going on in Los Angeles each week. Check one of the weekly newspapers (listed at the beginning of this chapter) for a full listing, or call the **Theatre LA Arts Hot line** at 213-688-2787. Listed below are some of the larger and/or more well-known theaters in Los Angeles.

- **Beverly Hills Playhouse,** 254 South Robertson, Beverly Hills, 310-855-1556
- **Canon Theatre,** 205 North Canon Drive, Beverly Hills, 310-859-2830
- **Doolittle Theatre,** 1615 North Vine Street, Hollywood, 213-972-7372
- **Will Geer Theatricum Botanicum,** 1419 North Topanga Canyon Boulevard, Topanga Canyon, 310-455-2322. Features Shakespeare and more, in a rustic, outdoor amphitheater.
- **Geffen Playhouse,** 10886 Le Conte Avenue, Westwood, 310-208-5454. Formerly the Westwood Playhouse, renamed due to a generous donation from entertainment mogul David Geffen.
- **The Music Center** (Dorothy Chandler Pavilion, Mark Taper Forum, and Ahmanson Theatre) 135 North Grand Avenue, Downtown, 213-972-7211
- **Odyssey Theatre Ensemble,** 2055 South Sepulveda Boulevard, West Los Angeles, 310-477-2055
- **Pantages Theatre,** 6233 Hollywood Boulevard, Hollywood, 213-468-1700
- **The Pasadena Playhouse,** 39 South El Molino Avenue, Pasadena, 818-356-PLAY
- **Santa Monica Playhouse,** 1211 4th Street, 310-394-9779
- **Shubert Theatre,** 2020 Avenue of the Stars, Century City, 310-201-1500
- **Tiffany Theatres,** 8532 Sunset Boulevard, West Hollywood, 310-289-2999

Amusement Parks

The Los Angeles area is home to several amusement parks, including the grand-daddy of them all, Disneyland. To avoid a shock to your wallet, you might want to call ahead to find out the various parks' admission and parking prices, which can be steep. Below is a list of the biggies:

- **Disneyland,** 1313 Harbor Boulevard, Anaheim, 714-999-4565. This is the original theme park, and the one that still seems to be held dearest in America's heart. Other parks may be bigger or have more thrilling rides, but most people agree that there is something special about bumping into Mickey Mouse as you walk down Main Street, U.S.A. Disneyland offers 55 different rides and attractions spread throughout seven different theme areas. It is open daily year-round, although seasonal hours vary.
- **Knott's Berry Farm,** 8039 Beach Boulevard, Buena Park, 714-220-5200. Knott's Berry Farm stretches across 150 acres, and offers more than 160 rides and attractions, as well as live performances. A Western theme pervades the park, which is open daily except Christmas.
- **Raging Waters,** 111 Raging Waters Drive, San Dimas, 909-592-6453. This 44-acre water park features rides, slides, sandy beaches, chutes and lagoons; in short, all different wild ways to cool off on a hot summer day. Raging Waters is open daily during the summer, weekends May and September through mid-October.
- **Santa Monica Pier,** at Ocean and Colorado Boulevards, Santa Monica, 310-458-8900. Though not really an amusement park, the Pier boasts carnival-style games and rides, a huge Ferris wheel, and a vintage carousel, all with an ocean view. Admission is free, though there are charges for the rides and games. Most attractions are open all day until 9:00 p.m. during the summer, and only on weekends during the rest of the year.
- **Six Flags Magic Mountain,** 26101 Magic Mountain Parkway, Valencia, 818-367-5965. This 260-acre amusement park offers an array of rides, attractions and shows. It is famous for its scary roller coasters including The Viper, the largest looping roller coaster in the world. Magic Mountain is open daily from Memorial Day to Labor Day, and school holidays and weekends during the rest of the year. Closed on Christmas.
- **Universal Studios Tour,** 100 Universal City Plaza, Universal City, 818-508-9600. Universal Studios offers a comprehensive tram ride tour throughout the studio grounds (with the possibility of star sightings!) and live action shows. Also at Universal City is a multiplex movie theater and Universal CityWalk, a three-block long shopping mall that is a mini-replica of Los Angeles.

O NCE you get settled, you may want to become involved in some of the many charitable organizations in Los Angeles. The list below is just a small sampling of the many worthy organizations and causes that would appreciate your support.

AIDS

AIDS Project Los Angeles (APLA), 213-962-1600
L.A. Shanti, 213-962-8197; 818-908-8849
Minority AIDS Project, 213-936-4949
Out of the Closet Thrift-Store, 213-466-7601
Stop AIDS LA, 213-957-5710
WomensCare Center, 213-662-7420

Alcohol and Drug Abuse

Alcoholics Anonymous, 310-836-8716
Cocaine Anonymous, 310-839-1141
Narcotics Anonymous, 310-390-0279
National Council on Alcoholism, 310-451-5881

Cancer

American Cancer Society, 310-670-2650
Lymphoma Research Foundation, 310-470-4912

Children

Big Brothers of Greater Los Angeles, 213-358-3333
Big Sisters of Los Angeles, 213-933-5749

Boy Scouts of America, 213-413-4400
Catholic Big Brothers, 800-453-KIDS
Girl Scouts of America, 213-933-4700
Interface Children, Family Services, 213-485-6114
Jewish Big Brothers, 800-453-KIDS
Juvenile Diabetes Foundation International, 310-842-6742
MidValley Youth Center, 818-904-0707
**School Volunteer Program of the Los Angeles Unified School
District,** 213-625-6900
Starlight Foundation of California, 310-286-0271

Disabilities

Association for Retarded Citizens, 213-290-2000
Braille Institute, 213-663-1111
Easter Seal Society of Los Angeles and Orange Counties, 310-204-
5533
Greater Los Angeles Council on Deafness, 213-383-2220
Orton/Ryan Center for Dyslexics, 213-748-9596
Westside Center for Independent Living, 310-390-3611

Environment

American Oceans Campaign, 310-576-6162
California Conservation Corps, 213-744-2254
Heal the Bay, 310-475-2994
Sierra Club, 213-387-4287

Food

The Salvation Army, 213-896-9160
SOVA Food Pantry, 310-828-3433
Westside Food Bank, 310-314-1150

Gay and Lesbian

Gay and Lesbian Alliance Against Defamation, 213-931-9429
Gay and Lesbian Parents of Los Angeles, 213-654-0307
Gay Center for Counseling, 818-783-0296

Health

Los Angeles Free Clinic, 213-653-8622
South Bay Free Clinic, 310-318-2521

Venice Family Clinic, 310-821-3484
Westside Hot Line, 310-226-7009

Homeless

Chrysalis, 213-895-7777
Habitat for Humanity, 818-765-2073
Saint Joseph Center, 310-399-6878
Step Up on Second, 310-395-8886

Legal

American Civil Liberties Union of Southern California, 213-977-9500
Bet Tzedek Legal Services, 213-939-0506
Westside Legal Services, 310-396-5456

Literacy

Southern California Literacy Hot line, 800-372-6641

Politics

Amnesty International, 310-815-0450
League of Women Voters of Los Angeles, 213-939-3535
Voter Registration, 213-721-1100

Seniors

American Association of Retired Persons, 310-496-2277
Jewish Family Services of Los Angeles, 213-937-5930
Retired Senior Volunteer Program, 213-461-4363, 310-559-5088
Senior Health and Peer Counseling, 310-828-1243

Women

Planned Parenthood of Los Angeles, 213-223-4462
Safe Harbor Women's Clinic, 213-744-3822
Santa Monica Hospital Rape Treatment Center, 310-319-4000
Venice Women's Clinic, 310-392-4147

THE excellent year-round weather in Los Angeles makes it a great place for athletes. For those who are fans as well as (or instead of) participants, once again, you've come to the right city. With two professional baseball teams, two professional basketball teams, a professional ice hockey team, and excellent local college athletics, sports enthusiasts can keep very busy here. True, the areas' former football teams, the Rams and the Raiders, are deserters. But rumor has it that it's only a matter of time before the Seattle Seahawks or another football team moves to L.A. In the meantime, there are plenty of other sporting events to keep your adrenaline pumping.

Professional Sports

Baseball

Baseball season runs from April through October.

The California Angels play at **Anaheim Stadium** (lovingly called "The Big A") in Orange County. While Disney recently purchased the team and as usual, has ambitious plans, don't expect to see mouse ears on the batting helmets any time soon. In the past the Angels had only sporadic success, but under the guidance of manager Marcel Lachemann and former Angel great and current hitting coach Rod Carew, a group of young up-and-comers and key veterans are hitting a ton and have turned the Angels into top contenders in the American League West. For ticket information, call 714-634-2000.

The Los Angeles Dodgers play at **Dodger Stadium** in Chavez Ravine, which was reportedly an Indian burial ground. The Dodgers last won the World Series in 1988 under the leadership of famous manager (eater, and dieter) Tommy Lasorda. As Fernando Valenzuela's pitching success in the early 80's drew a new crowd of fans to the park, the latest pitching sensation, Hideo Nomo from Japan has produced what is locally known as "Nomomania." On the days he pitches, it's common to find a crush of Japanese journalists in the press box, and California rolls served in the stands. Tickets for adults run from $5-$10, giving Dodger games the nickname "the cheapest ticket in town." For ticket information, call 213-224-1491.

Basketball

Basketball season picks up after baseball, and runs from October through April.

The Los Angeles Clippers play at the **LA Sports Arena** near USC. In this town, used to the Laker glory days of Magic Johnson and Kareem Abdul Jabbar, the Clippers were once treated like poor second cousins. Lately though, smart trades and fresh blood on the Clippers team have brought new fans into the fold, including the requisite celebrities court-side. For ticket information call 213-748-8000.

The Los Angeles Lakers play at **The Forum**, in Inglewood. Although the famed seasons of Magic Johnson, Kareem Abdul Jabbar, Wilt Chamberlain, Elgin Baylor and Jerry West are no longer, it's still "showtime at the Forum." If the game gets boring, you can check out the stars in the audience, since Dyan Cannon, Jack Nicholson, and other celebs are regulars. For ticket information, call 310-419-3100.

Hockey

The Los Angeles Kings play at **The Forum** in Inglewood. Ice hockey season begins in November and ends in March, unless as in 1993, the Kings make it to the Stanley Cup finals in June. "The Great One" Wayne Gretzky popularized hockey here in a city that only sees ice or snow on TV. As testimony to his popularity, these days you're as likely to see kids playing after-school street hockey games as sandlot baseball or touch football. Recently however, the news of the team's financial chaos and ownership changes has gotten more ink than the King's on-ice achievements. For ticket information, call 310-673-6003.

Horse Racing

There are three race tracks in the Los Angeles area.

- **Hollywood Park,** Inglewood, 310-419-1574. Races are run April through July, and November through December.
- **Los Angeles County Fairgrounds,** 909-623-3111. Races are run through the fair each September.
- **Santa Anita Park,** Arcadia, 818-574-RACE. Races are run October through November, and December through April.

Soccer

One of the legacies of the 1994 World Cup at Pasadena's Rose Bowl is the creation of Major League Soccer (MLS). MLS is the first attempt at a major soccer league since the NASL folded in 1993, and in the Spring of 1996, it will begin a Division 1 professional outdoor league in ten cities across the United States, including a franchise here in Los Angeles. The Los Angeles team is named the **LA Galaxy**, and will play at the **Rose Bowl**. Check that venue for more details.

Tennis

In August the **Infiniti Open** men's professional tournament is played at the Los Angeles Tennis Center at UCLA, and the **Toshiba Open** women's professional tournament is played at the Manhattan Beach Country Club. Both events draw some of the world's top players. For more information on either of the tournaments, contact the local United States Tennis Association office at 310-208-3838.

College Sports

With all the labor disputes in professional sports disrupting schedules and disillusioning fans, take heart that here in LA, fine local college games are plentiful, and dependable. In fact, enthusiasts of college-level sports may feel that living in LA is like dying and going to heaven, as the local schools consistently boast some of the nation's finest athletes and teams.

For instance, **UCLA's** basketball program is legendary, producing such phenoms as Kareem Abdul-Jabbar (then Lou Alcindor), Gail Goodrich, Jamaal (then Keith) Wilkes, Bill Walton, Marcus Johnson, Ann Meyers (sister of Dave), Reggie Miller and Ed O'Bannon. The football program is no slouch either, with former players on the roster like Troy Aikman and Ken Norton, and the home field being none other than the Rose Bowl. Likewise **USC** football can usually be described as nothing short of powerhouse, energized in the past by the likes of Mike Garrett, Charles White, Marcus Allen, Ricky Bell, Ronnie Lott, Junior Seau and yes, O.J. Simpson. Cheryl Miller, one of the greatest female basketball players ever, also was a Trojan.

Other local college sports programs of note are baseball at **Cal State Fullerton, Pepperdine's** tennis and water polo, **Loyola Marymount** for basketball (where the tragic death of their player Hank Gathers took place), **Long Beach State's** basketball, UCLA's volleyball, gymnastics, softball, and water polo, and USC's water polo, as well.

For athletic ticket information, call the following numbers:

- **Cal State Fullerton,** 714-773-2187
- **Loyola Marymount,** 310-338-4532
- **Long Beach State,** 310-985-4949
- **Pepperdine,** 310-456-4150
- **UCLA,** 310-825-2101
- **USC,** 213-740-4672

Participant Sports

Basketball

Pick-up basketball games are available all over the city. In some places you'll find friendly games, and at others competition is fierce. The movie "White Men Can't Jump" showed off the busy pick-up basketball scene at Venice's Boardwalk. While it may look like this is the spot with the best and flashiest players in town, there are good games to be found all over, from school yards to city parks. The Wooden Center's indoor courts at UCLA are where the "big names" show up, and it's not uncommon for hot college players, former professionals, or even a current pro to drop by for a game of pick-up.

Bicycling

Both tour bicycling and mountain bicycling are very popular in Los Angeles. The most traveled bike path is the **coastal bike path** from **Pacific Palisades** in the north to **Torrance** in the south. The path looks like a bicycling and skating freeway during the weekends. If you don't have a bike of your own, rentals are available at several shacks down on the beach in **Marina del Rey, Venice** and **Santa Monica.** Other popular trails include the **Ballona Creek Trail,** and the **Pasadena bike trail.**

Mountain bikers enjoy the challenging trails in the **Santa Monica mountains,** including **Sullivan Canyon** along (and through) the creek bed, the **Malibu Canyon trails, Topanga State Park** (310-455-2465), and **Sycamore Canyon.**

For more information about area routes, call the **Los Angeles County Transportation Commission** at (213) 236-9555.

For bicycling equipment and other information, here are some of the more popular cycling stores:

- **Bikeology**
  Beverly Hills, 9006 West Pico Boulevard, 310-278-0915
  Marina del Rey, 4224 Lincoln Boulevard, 310-821-0766

- **Helen's Cycles**
  Manhattan Beach, 1570 Rosecrans Avenue, 310-643-9140
  Marina del Rey, 2472 Lincoln Boulevard, 310-306-7843
  Santa Monica, 2501 Broadway, 310-829-1836
  Westwood, 1071 Gayley Avenue, 310-208-8988

Billiards/Pool

Pool possibilities here run the gamut from lone tables in the middle of seedy bars, to old-fashioned smoky billiard halls, to the trendy pool halls of late. Here are a few for you to sample:

- **Gotham Hall,** 1431 Third Street Promenade, Santa Monica, 310-394-8865
- **Hollywood Athletic Club,** 6525 Sunset Boulevard, 213-962-6600
- **Hollywood Athletic Club,** Universal CityWalk, 818-505-9238
- **House of Billiards,** 1901 Wilshire Boulevard, Santa Monica.
- **LA Society Billiard Cafe,** 19626 Ventura Boulevard, Tarzana, 818-344-POOL
- **Q's,** 11835 Wilshire Boulevard, Brentwood, 310-477-7550
- **Stick & Stein Eatery and Sports Parlor,** 707 Sepulveda Boulevard, El Segundo, 310-414-9283
- **Yankee Doodles,** 1410 Third Street Promenade, Santa Monica, 310-394-4632

Boating

Marina del Rey is the spot for most boating activity in the Santa Monica Bay. Aside from the private sail boats, speed boats, and plain old yachts moored in the Marina, several companies offer sailing lessons and rentals.

- **Bluewater Sailing,** 13505 Bali Way, Marina del Rey, 310-823-5545
- **Pacific Sailing,** 14110 Marquesas Way, Marina del Rey, 310-823-4064
- **Rent-A-Sail,** 13719 Fiji Way, Marina del Rey, 310-822-1868

Bowling

- **Active West** operates 21 modern bowling facilities in Southern California. Call 213-879-5791 for the one nearest you, or try one of the two below:
- **Bay Shore Bowl,** 234 Pico Boulevard, Santa Monica, 310-399-7731
- **Hollywood Star Lanes,** 5227 Santa Monica Boulevard, Hollywood, 213-665-4111. 24-hour bowling, and cocktails served until 2 a.m.

• **Mar Vista Bowl,** 12125 Venice Boulevard, West Los Angeles, 310-391-5288

Golf

There are more than 100 **public golf courses** in the Greater Los Angeles area. The City of Los Angeles operates seven 18-hole courses, and five 9-hole courses. For information, call 213-485-5555. The County of Los Angeles operates 16 courses; for information call, 213-738-2961. Be forewarned, golf is very popular here, so book a tee-time well in advance.

• **Eaton Canyon Golf Course,** 1150 North Sierra Madre Villa Avenue, Pasadena, 818-794-6773. This is a 30-year-old, 2,900 yard, 9-hole layout featuring two par fives.
• **Holmby Park Golf Course,** 601 Club View Drive, Westwood, 310-276-1604. This is an 18-hole pony golf course, 3-par.
• **Malibu Golf Course,** 901 Encinal Canyon Road, Malibu, 818-889-6680. There is one 18-hole golf course here.
• **Penmar Golf Course,** 1223 Rose Avenue, Venice, 310-396-6228. Penmar features one 9-hole course.
• **Rancho Park Golf Course,** 10460 Pico Boulevard, West Los Angeles, 310-838-7373. Rancho is billed as one of the busiest golf courses in the country. It features an 18-hole course, plus a par three 9-hole pitch-n-putt.
• **Roosevelt Golf Course,** 2650 North Vermont Avenue, Los Angeles, 213-665-2011. Roosevelt features one 9-hole course.
• **Sepulveda Basin Recreational Area,** Burbank and Balboa Boulevards, Encino, 310-989-8060. There are two 18-hole golf courses at this 60-acre wildlife refuge.

Hiking

The **Santa Monica** and **San Gabriel Mountains** provide miles of varied hiking trails. The following are local state parks offering hiking trails:

• **Coldwater Canyon Park,** 818-753-4600. Located along the southern slope of the Santa Monica Mountains, this park offers five-plus miles of hiking trails.
• **Elysian Park,** 213-225-2044. Located in **Echo Park,** Elysian offers more than ten miles of hiking trails, winding through forested hills and green valleys.
• **Griffith Park,** 213-665-5188. There are 35 miles of hiking trails in this vast park above Hollywood.
• **Malibu Creek State Park,** 310-880-0350. More than 15 miles of hiking trails weave through this mostly undeveloped park.

- **Santa Monica Mountains National Recreation Area,** 818-597-1036. The Santa Monica Mountains stretch almost 50 miles across Los Angeles. This area includes **Will Rogers State Historic Park** (310-454-8212), the 31-room former ranch home of actor, humorist, and columnist Will Rogers and the miles of trails behind his house. Most of the trails in the Santa Monica Mountains are part of, or hook up to, the Backbone Trail.
- **Temescal Gateway Park,** 310-756-7154. This 20-acre park includes a trail that travels more than 12 miles north to the **Backbone Trail.**
- **Topanga State Park,** 310-455-2465. This 10,000-acre park offers 32 miles of hiking trails.

The county now requires that anyone using LA County nature trails purchase a $23 annual pass. City, state, and federal trails are still free. There are about 330 miles of country trails in Los Angeles, including the following trails: **Frank G. Bonnell Regional Park Trail, San Dimas; Schabarum Trail,** from Whittier to Rowland Heights; **Colby Dalton Trail,** Glendora; **Altadena Crest Trail,** Altadena; **La Canada Open Space Trail,** La Canada Flintridge; **Los Angeles River Trail,** from Downey to Long Beach; **Devil's Punchbowl Nature Trail,** Antelope Valley; **Los Pinetos Trail,** Sylmar; **Coastal Slope Trail,** Malibu; and **Eaton Canyon Park Trail,** Pasadena. The fine for using the above-listed trails without a permit is $100.

Horseback Riding

Several areas offer horseback riding rentals, lessons, and/or boarding, including the following:

- **Red Barn Stables,** Malibu, 818-879-0444, or toll-free 800-300-0968. Offers beach rides.
- **Sunset Ranch Hollywood Stables,** 213-469-5450. Offers moonlight rides through Hollywood Hills and Griffith Park.

Ice Skating

If ice skating is your sport, try one of the following rinks, which also offer lessons:

- **Culver City Ice Arena,** 4545 Sepulveda Boulevard, 310-398-5718
- **Ice Capades Chalet,** 6100 Laurel Canyon Boulevard, North Hollywood, 818-985-5555

In-line Skating (and traditional Skating)

The parks and beaches of Los Angeles are bustling with in-line skating (popularly known as Rollerblading™), and regular skating, too. Rentals can be found at several shacks along the coastal path, in **Marina del Rey, Venice,** and **Santa Monica.** Beware, bicyclists and skaters turn the bike path into a veritable Autobahn on weekends. There are also the traditional skating rinks, like those listed below:

- **World on Wheels,** 4645 1/2 Venice Boulevard, Los Angeles, 213-933-3333
- **Moonlight Rollerway,** 5110 San Fernando Road, Glendale, 818-241-3630

Paddle Tennis

Those aren't kiddie-sized tennis courts you see dotting the beaches along the bike path, they're paddle tennis courts. Paddle tennis is similar to tennis, but it is played on a smaller court with deadened tennis balls and paddles, rather than rackets. You can try your talent for this popular game at one of the following spots:

- **415 PCH,** Santa Monica, 310-458-8555. There are five paddle tennis courts located just off the beach at this former private club.
- **Culver City,** 310-202-5689. There are three courts at the corner of Culver and Elenda.
- **Venice Recreational Center,** 310-399-2775. There are eight paddle tennis courts located right on the beach.

Running

The miles along the beach on the coastal path provide a beautiful setting for runners. Another popular Westside running spot is the median park strip on **San Vicente Boulevard,** starting in Brentwood and continuing through Santa Monica to the cliffs above the ocean. In the Hollywood area, the path around the **Hollywood Reservoir** (also known as Lake Hollywood) provides a nice place to jog.

Some Santa Monica runners like to include in their loop a strenuous staircase that runs from the end of 4th Street north of San Vicente Boulevard, and leads into Santa Monica Canyon. In fact, many people bike or drive over to this spot, specifically to trod up and down these 200 steep steps, known as the **4th Street stairs.** Aside from a beautiful ocean vista and a good workout, the stairs also provide an active social scene, particularly on weekends when it gets downright crowded. But if you want to give the steps a try, watch your manners. Climbers look down on perfume or cologne wearing, which interferes with their huffing and puffing, and don't mess with the stones and other markers at the top and bottom of the steps, which help exercises keep track of how many flights they have completed. Also, recently neighbors in this tony area have complained that some climbers walk or sit on their front lawns, leave empty water bottles around, or even use their hoses to cool off, so be considerate and follow the Golden Rule.

The Los Angeles Marathon gathers more than 20,000 competitors each March at the Los Angeles Memorial Coliseum. The course runs through Chinatown, Hollywood, and Echo Park. For more information, call 310-444-5544. For novice runners who have never accomplished a marathon or active runners who want to train with a group, the **LA Leggers** has a $35, 30-week training program in preparation for the LA Marathon. The telephone number for LA Leggers is 310-450-3915.

Scuba Diving

Many private scuba schools as well as departments of parks and recreation offer scuba (which stands for self-contained underwater breathing apparatus) instruction. While the diving in the **Santa Monica Bay** doesn't offer the greatest visibility, day trips to **Catalina Island** and **The Channel Islands** near Santa Barbara offer divers some beautiful and exciting dives. Plus, if you are interested in diving with marine mammals like seals and sea lions, the California coast is the place. Here are a few of the many dive shops/schools in the area; check your telephone directory under "Diving Instruction" for others.

- **Blue Cheer Dive & Surf,** 1110 Wilshire Boulevard, Santa Monica, 310-828-1217
- **Malibu Divers,** 21231 Pacific Coast Highway, Malibu, 310-456-2396
- **Pacific School of Scuba,** 9763 West Pico Boulevard, West Los Angeles, 310-286-7377
- **Reef Seekers,** 8612 Wilshire Boulevard, Beverly Hills, 310-652-4990

Softball

There are numerous softball leagues throughout Los Angeles, many of which are organized through workplace. There is, for instance, an advertising league and a law league. Ask your colleagues, or call your department of parks and recreation for more information.

Soccer

As a city with a large and growing Latino population, soccer is a popular otpage.

sport in Los Angeles. Balboa Park is North Hollywood is known as a site of a weekly, organized matches between multi-ethnic club teams. Check your phone directory under "Soccer Clubs" for more information.

Surfing

Dude, you can catch some totally gnarly waves here in Los Angeles. Seriously, surfing is a major part of the beach culture in Southern California, and all along the LA coastline there are beaches and coves where surfing reigns supreme. For information on where to surf, contact the **Department of Beaches & Harbors**, at 310-305-9503. To buy a surfboard, check the telephone directory under "Surf Boards." To learn how to surf, you can drive up to Malibu for an afternoon, watch the veterans, then grab a board and give it a try. Trial by fire may be the most popular teaching method, but keep in mind that the locals can be territorial, and newcomers aren't always welcomed with open arms. If you have a buddy who already surfs, you might be better off letting him/her show you the ropes.

Before you head out, here are the numbers to call for surfing conditions: **Central Section,** 310-451-8761; **Northern Section,** 310-457-9701; **San Pedro-Cabrillo Beach Section,** 310-832-1130; **Southern Section,** 310-379-8471.

Swimming

There are several places you can go to swim in Los Angeles. Many **YMCAs** offer use of their pool for a fee, as do several city-run parks and recreation facilities, such as the ones listed below. All are open year-round.

- **Echo Park Indoor Pool,** (One indoor Olympic, one outdoor shallow) 1419 Colton Street, Echo Park, 213-481-2640
- **Fremont Pool** (indoor), 7630 Towne Avenue, Los Angeles, 213-847-3401
- **The Plunge,** 219 West Mariposa Avenue, El Segundo, 310-322-1677
- **Rancho Cienega Pool** (indoor), 5001 Rodeo Road, Los Angeles, 213-847-3406
- **Eleanor G. Roberts Pool** (indoor), 4526 West Pico Boulevard, Los Angeles, 213-936-8483
- **Roosevelt Pool** (Olympic size, outdoor), 456 South Mathews, Los Angeles, 213-485-7391
- **Westwood Recreation Complex,** 1350 Sepulveda Boulevard, Westwood, 310-473-3610
- **Venice Pool** (indoor), 2401 Walgrove Avenue, Venice, 310-575-8260

Unfortunately, the **Santa Monica Bay** has suffered from pollution at the hands of Los Angelenos. Efforts to clean it up are underway, and the bay is actually cleaner now than in years past, but there are often swimming advisories near the major storm drains. If you want to swim in the ocean, you might want to head up to **Malibu.**

Tennis

Year-round outdoor tennis is one of the many benefits of the good weather here. There are public tennis courts throughout the city, and on some you pay a small fee in exchange for the ability to make a court reservation. Also, these pay-to-play courts are often in better condition than other public courts. Following are some of the more popular public tennis spots:

- **Echo Park,** Echo Park, six courts, 213-250-3578
- **La Cienega Park,** Beverly Hills, fourteen courts, 310-550-4625
- **Lincoln Park,** Santa Monica, six courts, 310-394-6011
- **Plummer Park,** West Hollywood, six courts, 213-876-1725
- **Westwood Recreation Complex,** Westwood, six courts, 310-473-3610

Volleyball

Several beaches offer beach volleyball courts, including **Zuma, Malibu Lagoon, Will Rogers, Santa Monica State**, **Venice,** and **Manhattan,** which has more than 100 courts. Additionally, many parks have volleyball courts, including the **West Wilshire Recreation Center** (213-939-8874), **Palisades Recreation Center** (310-454-1412), **Barrington Recreation Center** (310-476-3807), and **Westwood Recreation Complex** (310-473-3610).

Health Clubs

LA is the fabled land of "the beautiful people", and you too may notice that physiques seem trimmer and fitter here than elsewhere in the country. The good weather makes it nice to exercise outdoors, but people here also work out at health clubs, in record numbers.

There are **YMCAs** located throughout the city (check the telephone directory for one near you), and many offer good workout options at reasonable prices. On the other end of the spectrum, the most luxurious fitness complex in town is **The Sports Club LA** (310-473-1447), which offers everything from personal trainers to a gourmet grill restaurant.

Here are some health clubs that fall in-between:

- **Bally's Holiday Spa Health Clubs** are located throughout the city. For the one nearest you, call 800-695-8111.
- **Family Fitness Centers** have 11 sites in the Los Angeles area. Check the telephone directory under "Health Clubs" for one nearest you.
- **The Sports Connection** health clubs are located in Santa Monica (310-829-6836), West Hollywood (310-652-7440) and West Los Angeles (310-450-4464).

Departments of Parks and Recreation

For information on park facilities, leagues, clubs, and lessons, contact any of the below listed departments of parks and recreation:

- **Beverly Hills Recreation Department,** 310-285-2537
- **Culver City Recreation Department,** 310-202-5689
- **El Segundo Parks and Recreation Department,** 310-322-3842
- **Los Angeles Recreation and Parks Department,** 213-485-5555
- **Malibu Parks and Recreation Department,** 310-456-2489, extension 235
- **Manhattan Beach Recreation Department,** 310-545-5621, extension 325
- **Pasadena Parks and Recreation Department,** 818-405-4306
- **Santa Monica Recreation Division,** 310-458-8311
- **West Hollywood Recreation Department,** 310-854-7471

LOS ANGELES gets much notoriety for its urban sprawl. What may be less evident, until you live here, is that this area is rich in green, open spaces like parks, both urban and rural, and of course, beaches.

Green Space

Urban parks dot the city, offering things like tennis courts, baseball diamonds, basketball courts, and plenty of grass to stretch out and relax. For a listing of the parks in your neighborhood, check the front section of your telephone book, or call the recreation and parks department for your area (see previous page).Two of the largest urban parks in Los Angeles are Griffith Park and Cheviot Hills.

Located in the Hollywood Hills, **Griffith Park** is the largest publicly owned park in the United States. It occupies 4,400 acres in the hills, and features the Los Angeles Zoo, the Griffith Park Observatory Planetarium and Laserium, Travel Town train park, and the Autry Museum of Western Heritage. There are also pony rides, tennis courts, a soccer field, merry-go-round, picnic areas, and 50 miles of hiking and horseback riding trails.

Cheviot Hills Park, located in West Los Angeles near Cheviot Hills, offers 14 lit tennis courts and pro shop, archery, swimming, basketball courts, soccer fields, baseball diamonds, a par course, a driving range, and what is reputed to be one of the busiest public golf courses in the country, Rancho Park.

If you're looking to be near some water but don't want to head for the beach, **Silverlake** and **Echo Park** are nice places to cool off and relax, or take a jog or a walk around the lakes. At Echo Park you can rent canoes or paddle boats, or utilize the tennis courts, baseball diamonds, and two pools, one indoor Olympic-sized and one outdoor that is shallow. Since the lake is usually stocked, fishing is available, too.

Silverlake is actually a reservoir, so no water access is allowed, but it still makes for a pretty, calming site, and the park does offer basketball courts, playing fields, and a gymnasium for children. And, nestled beneath the famed Hollywood sign is **Lake Hollywood**, which is not really a lake at all but an irrigated flood control area. Nonetheless, it features much open space, a jogging path around the lake that is strictly for pedestrian traffic, and a children's play area.

For those times when you can plan ahead, a visit to the **UCLA Hannah Carter Japanese Garden** (310-825-4574) in the hills of Bel Air is a restful excursion. Open to the public only two afternoons per week, reservations are required and visits are supervised. But if you can tolerate all those provisos, you'll be treated to ancient pagodas, devil-casting stones, wild boar scarers, and a mix of indigenous Japanese trees and plants. If botanical gardens are your cup of tea, you should also consider the **Huntington Library and Gardens** (818-405-2141) in Pasadena, the **Virginia Robinson Gardens** (310-276-5367) in Beverly Hills, and the **Los Angeles County Arboretum** (818-821-3211) in Arcadia.

The canyon parks offer a much different experience: the chance to drive only a short distance yet leave the city behind. A few minutes along a hiking trail can find you in a spot where cars can't be heard and houses can't be seen, and you're about as likely to meet up with a lizard or jackrabbit as a human being.

The largest area of canyon parkland is incorporated into the **Santa Monica Mountains National Recreation Area**. The Santa Monica Mountains stretch almost 50 miles across Los Angeles. Most of the trails in the Santa Monica Mountains are part of, or hook up to, the **Backbone Trail**. For more information about parks throughout these mountains, call 818-597-1036.

Located on the northeastern edge of the San Fernando Valley is **Angeles National Forest**, one of seventeen national forests in California. Though accessible at many different points, the nearest part of the forest to most Los Angeles residents in adjacent to Pasadena, in the **San Gabriel Mountains**. Here you'll find campgrounds, picnic sites, lakes, streams, and miles of hiking trails. For more information call 818-574-5200.

Nestled in the Santa Monica Mountains near Pacific Palisades is **Will Rogers State Historic Park**. The former ranch of actor, humorist, and columnist Will Rogers, the park features tours through the 31-room former ranch home, a large grassy hill for picnics, and miles of trails behind the house. On weekend mornings you can sit alongside the polo field and watch the horses race by during matches.

Other beautiful canyon parks are **Malibu Creek State Park,** with more than 15 miles of hiking trails, **Temescal Gateway Park,** a 20-acre site that includes a trail that travels more than 12 miles north to the Backbone Trail, and **Topanga State Park,** with 10,000-acres and 32 miles of hiking trails. In the Spring these parks are filled with wildflowers that make hiking a colorful experience.

Beaches

Of course, Los Angeles is famous for its beaches, and they too provide an alluring place to get away from it all. There's nothing quite like standing at the edge of the continent, comforted by the knowledge that although there may be millions of people and a bustling civilization behind you, there are no such distractions in front of you as far as your eyes can see.

A few words of safety advice about going to the beach: First, if you plan on swimming, stay in front of the nearest open lifeguard tower on the beach. Second, take care to protect your eyes and skin. The sun's strong rays can not only harm your appearance by way of sunburns and wrinkles, but they can cause eyesight impairment and skin cancer. Don't follow the example of those leatherette lovelies who bake all day in the sun; cover up with UV-safe glasses, hats, or clothing if necessary, and use sunscreen. Third, being alone or even in a small group on the beach after dark is unfortunately not a safe idea. Stick to beach combing as a daytime activity.

At Malibu's most northwestern end is **Leo Carillo State Beach,** named for an LA-born actor. The 1,600-acre beach features nature trails leading to tide pools, and three campgrounds. The water is good for surfing and swimming, and you can explore Sequit Point which has sea caves and a natural tunnel.

Further southeast is **Zuma Beach,** known for its scenic views and rough surf. Zuma features volleyball, swimming, surfing, fishing, diving, and a kid's playground. At nearby **Point Dume** you can explore tide pools, and perhaps catch the migrating California gray whales, which travel through the area from November through May. Malibu's **Surfrider Beach** is known for its surfing as the name implies, but also has volleyball courts and a marine preserve with tide pools and a nature center.

At the foot of Topanga Canyon are the small **Las Tunas State Beach** and **Topanga State Beach**. Though Topanga covers almost 22 acres, it is most populated at a mile-long sandy stretch near Topanga Creek. Further south is **Will Rogers State Beach,** a popular spot for surfing, bodysurfing, and swimming. It too has volleyball courts, as well as a diving area and a playground.

Santa Monica State Beach is one of the largest and most popular beaches in California, due to its close location to much of the city, and amusement amenities like the Santa Monica Pier, playgrounds, and basketball and volleyball courts. Though you will see many people swimming here, reports on the water quality at local beaches often rate this one poorly. If you do choose to swim, stay away from storm drains and the areas closest to the pier.

Venice Beach features 238-acres of sand, but it's the adjacent boardwalk (see "Venice" under "Neighborhoods" section) that has made it famous and brings most visitors. Bicycles can be rented at several vendors along the beach front, and there's a nice kid's playground. This is not the beach to visit to escape humanity, but for great people-watching, it can't be beat.

Marina del Rey's **Dockweiler Beach** is quieter, though popular with families and young, single professionals. Features here include three-miles of shoreline, swimming, surfing, a picnic area and a campground. Busy **Manhattan Beach** boasts more than 100 volleyball courts. One of the main attractions here is The Strand, a concrete promenade for jogging, skating, and walking.

For a long day-trip or an over-nighter, you might like to check out **Catalina Island**, which can be spied on a clear day off-shore. "Twenty-two miles across the sea, Santa Catalina is waiting for me," goes a famous old song, which later refers to the place as "island of romance". The only town there Avalon, which features the islands' hotel, motel, and bed & breakfast accommodations, along with shops and restaurants. There's also camping available outside of town, as well as good hiking, bicycling, and scuba diving. There are no cars on Catalina, so locals tool around in golf carts, and you can, too. To get to the island, the skilled and equipped can sail over themselves, or you can arrive via ferry or helicopter. For more information, call the Catalina Island Chamber of Commerce at 310-510-1520.

By Car

A QUICK GLANCE at a map will tell you that Los Angeles is the land of freeways. Any way you look at it, morning and afternoon rush hours are a bear. Try to avoid them, but if you must, heed the "Sig-Alerts" (named after their inventor), the electronic freeway condition signs that tell you where major delays can be expected.

In general, the freeways are still the best way to go long distances. I-5 is the interstate freeway that runs north-south, and is the fastest, though not the prettiest route to the San Francisco Bay Area and other parts of Northern California. US 101 is a more scenic route through the state, and cuts through the San Fernando Valley and Hollywood. Highway 1, known as the Pacific Coast Highway (PCH) in the Los Angeles area, runs up and down the entire California coastline. Most agree that at one time or another, it's worth the extra hours on the road to take Highway 1 to or from Northern California, as it covers some of the most beautiful geography in the country.

Locally, I-10 runs east-west, and is the major way to get from West Los Angeles to Downtown, and points in between. The 405 goes between The Valley and West Los Angeles, and down through the South Bay, and can have punishing traffic, so be forewarned.

Most locals have their tried and true shortcuts around town (remember Steve Martin's cruise through alleys, parking lots, and front lawns in "LA Story"?), but they may be stingy about telling you what they are. After all, too much traffic on the shortcuts defeats the purpose! It's worth experimenting yourself to see which byways move and which don't.

Car Rental

There are numerous car rental agencies near the airports, and throughout the city. Call the following phone numbers for information, reservations, and locations:

- **Alamo,** 800-327-9633
- **Avis,** 12 locations, 800-831-2847
- **Budget,** 8 locations, 800-527-0700
- **Dollar,** 800-800-4000
- **Enterprise,** 15 locations, 800-325-8007
- **Hertz,** 800-654-3131
- **National,** 800-227-7368
- **Payless,** 800-729-5377
- **Rent-a-Wreck,** 800-535-1391
- **Thrifty,** 800-367-2277

Taxis and Shuttles

Unlike New York or Chicago, Los Angeles is not a major taxi town. You will not, for instance, be able to step out of any building and flag down a cab. Nonetheless, there are taxis outside the airports, hotels, and tourist attractions. If you need a cab at a specific time, your best bet is to call and order one in advance. Group shuttles are almost always cheaper than cabs for one passenger, and may still be cheaper for groups. The listing below includes both taxis and shuttles.

- **Airport Shuttle,** 310-971-8265
- **Checker Cab,** 310-201-0307
- **Super Shuttle,** 310-381-1111 (For group airport transport)
- **Yellow Cab,** 310-273-5528
- **Yellow Taxi,** 310-201-0004

Limousines

Check the telephone directory under "Limousine" for a listing of the many companies that provide limo service.

By Public Transportation

Los Angeles has an interesting history with public transportation. Until the 1940's, LA had an extensive system of electric cars, known as "Red Cars." The original tracks can still be seen in Santa Monica, Beverly Hills, and other parts of the city. Pressure from automobile companies and others led to the demise of the system, and the story is now one of the region's great scandals. Recently, civic leaders have begun to rectify the situation, and **The Metrorail** is the first step. The new train system connects several destinations to Downtown. The **Blue Line** runs from

Downtown to Long Beach, while the **Red Line** runs West from Union Station about one mile, and will eventually go further. Even so, most residents using public transportation still use buses to get around. Here is the lowdown on bus travel:

- **The Culver City Bus** can be reached by calling 310-559-8310 for recorded information. It provides local service in Culver City and to Los Angeles, Los Angeles International Airport (LAX), Marina del Rey, UCLA, Venice and the Westside. The adult fare is 60¢.
- **The Santa Monica Municipal Bus Lines (Big Blue Bus)** can be reached at 310-451-5444. The Big Blue Bus services Santa Monica and the Westside, and some routes extend to UCLA, LAX, and downtown.
- **The Southern California Rapid Transit District (RTD)** serves the Greater LA area, with more than 200 bus, rail and light-rail routes. Call 310-273-0910 or 213-626-4455 for more information.
- **The Downtown DASH** buses take two routes through the center of Downtown for a flat fee of 25¢.

For information on commuter carpools and vanpools, call **Commuter Transportation Services** at 213-380-7433. For door-to-door transportation referrals for seniors and mobility-impaired people, call **Info Line Paratransit Referral Service** at 818-350-8959. For more information on transportation around the greater LA area, call the **Regional Transportation Information Network** at 800-2LA-RIDE.

Amtrak

Amtrak can be reached at 800-872-7245. The Los Angeles station is **Union Station,** and is located downtown at 800 North Alameda Street, 213-624-0171.

By Airline

- **Los Angeles International Airport (LAX)** is the largest and busiest airport on the West Coast. It is located on the coast, just south of Playa del Rey. For information, call 310-646-5252.
- **Burbank Airport** is located at 2627 North Hollywood Way, 818-840-8847. Many smaller airlines and shorter flights (to Northern California, for instance) fly directly in and out of Burbank.
- **Long Beach Airport** is located at 4100 E. Donald Douglas Drive, 310-421-8295. For information on parking, call 310-425-9665.

- **Ontario International Airport** is located southeast of Los Angeles, at Airport Drive and Vineyard Avenue in Ontario. For general information, call 909-988-2700, for parking information call 909-988-2737.
- **Orange County's John Wayne Airport** is located at 18741 Airport Way in Santa Ana, 714-252-5006, parking 714-252-6262.

S A CITY with a huge tourism industry, Los Angeles and the surrounding areas have numerous hotels and motels. Accommodations run the gamut from utilitarian to ultra-luxurious. When reserving a room, be sure to ask about discounts or weekend packages. Some hotels offer senior citizen rates. Many lodgings have un-advertised special rates that they offer only if customers inquire. Keep in mind that summer rates can be higher than the rest of the year, and that big conventions or other events will cause hotels to fill up fast and rates to rise. Remember, the cost of living is high in Los Angeles, and hotel room rates reflect that fact.

The following list of hotels and motels is by no means complete. For more listings, check the telephone directory under "Hotels and Motels". If you know the area in which you wish to book a room, you might call the local Chamber of Commerce for a list of what's available.

Inexpensive Lodgings

- **Comfort Inn,** 2815 Santa Monica Boulevard, Santa Monica, 310-828-5517. Room prices start at $65.
- **Holiday Inn,** 800-465-4329. There are approximately 25 Holiday Inns in the Los Angeles area. Call for reservations and information.
- **Howard Johnson,** 800-654-2000. There are five Howard Johnson's in the Los Angeles area. Call for reservations and information.

Medium-Priced Lodgings

- **Marriott Hotels,** 800-288-9290. Marriotts are located in Century City, Long Beach, LAX, Marina del Rey, Torrance, and Woodland Hills. Call for rates and reservations, prices vary according to location.

- **Radisson Huntley Hotel,** 1111 Second Street, Santa Monica, 310-394-5454. Rooms start at $89.
- **Ramada West Hollywood,** 8585 Santa Monica Boulevard, West Hollywood, 310-652-6400. Rooms start at $95.
- **Shangri-La,** 1301 Ocean Avenue, Santa Monica, 310-394-2791. Rooms start at $110.
- **Wyndham Checkers Hotel,** 535 South Grand Avenue, Downtown, 213-624-0000. Rooms start at $109 on weekends.

Luxury Lodgings

There is no shortage of luxury hotels in Los Angeles. Here are just a few of the many:

- **The Argyle,** 8358 Sunset Boulevard, West Hollywood, 213-654-7100. Rooms starts at $175.
- **Beverly Hills Hotel,** 9641 Sunset Boulevard, Beverly Hills, 310- 276-2251. Rooms start at $275.
- **Hotel Bel Air,** 701 Stone Canyon Road, Bel Air, 310-472-1211. Rooms start at $315.
- **Loews Santa Monica Beach Hotel,** 1700 Ocean Avenue, 310-458-6700. Rooms start at $205, without an ocean view.
- **Regent Beverly Wilshire,** 9500 Wilshire Boulevard, Beverly Hills, 310-275-5200. Rooms start at $255.
- **Ritz Carlton Huntington,** 1401 South Oak Knoll Avenue, Pasadena, 818-568-3900. Rooms start at $165.
- **Ritz Carlton Marina del Rey,** 4375 Admiralty Way, Marina del Rey, 310-823-1700. Rooms start at $225.

Hostels

There are three **American Youth Hostels** in the Los Angeles area. They are:

- Santa Monica, 1434 2nd Street, 310-393-3413
- Fullerton, 1700 North Harbor Boulevard (nearest to Disneyland), 714-738-3721
- San Pedro, 3601 South Gaffey Street, #613, 310-831-8109

Bed & Breakfast

- **Channel Road Inn,** 219 Channel Road, Santa Monica, 310-459-1920

• **San Vicente Inn,** 837 North San Vicente Boulevard, West Hollywood, 310-854-6915

Short-Term Leases

• **Oakwood Apartments**
Marina del Rey, 4111 Via Marina, 310-823-5443
Los Angeles, 209 South Westmoreland, 213-380-4421
West Los Angeles, 3636 South Sepulveda Boulevard, 310-398-2794

YMCA

• **The Hollywood YMCA** at 1553 North Schrader (213-467-4161) is the only local Y that offers lodging. Dormitory rooms are $15 per night.

Call 911 for all police, fire and ambulance emergencies.

Alcohol and Drug Abuse

Alcoholics Anonymous 310-474-7339
Cocaine Anonymous 310-839-1141
Los Angeles County Office of Alcohol Programs 213-744-6500
Narcotics Anonymous 310-390-0279
National Alcohol and Drug Abuse Hot line 800-252-6465

Animals

Society for the Prevention of Cruelty to Animals 213-730-5300
Animal Regulations Department, City of Los Angeles 310 820-2691
Dead Animal Pick-up, City of Los Angeles 213-575-8392
Santa Monica Animal Shelter 310-458-8594

Birth and Death Certificates

Los Angeles County Clerk 310-462-2137

City of Los Angeles

Mayor's Office 213-485-3311

Child Abuse and Family Violence

Child Abuse Hotline 800-540-4000

```
Childhelp USA ............................... .800-422-4453
Children's Home Society of California ............... .213-482-5443
Elder Abuse Hot line .......................... .800-992-1660
Sojourn Services for Battered Women ............... .310-399-9239
```

Consumer Complaints and Services

```
Better Business Bureau ......................... .213-251-9696
Complaints, Better Business Bureau ................ .714-527-0680
State of California Consumer Affairs Department ...... .213-620-4360
U.S. Consumer Product Safety Commission .......... .800-638-2772
```

Crime

```
Crime in Progress ........................................ .911
Crime Prevention, Santa Monica ................... .310-458-8473
```

Crisis Hotlines

```
Poison Control Center ......................... .800-777-6476
Suicide Prevention ............................ .213-381-5111
Battered Women Hotline ........................ .310-392-9896
```

Elected Officials

```
Los Angeles County Board of Supervisors ........... .213-974-3333
Mayor's Office ................................ .213-485-3311
```

Housing

```
California State Fairness Employment and
Housing Department ........................... .213-620-2610
Community Cooperation of Santa Monica ............ .310-394-8487
Homeowners and Renters Assistance ............... .800-852-5711
Santa Monica Housing Authority ................... .310-458-8740
U.S. Department of Fair Housing and
Discrimination Hot line ......................... .800-424-8590
```

Information

```
Highway Conditions ........................... .213-628-7623
```

Smog Conditions 800-242-4022
Time 853-1212
Voter Information 213-721-1100
Weather 213-554-1212
Zip Codes 213-586-1737, 800-894-3433

Rape Crisis Hotlines

Los Angeles County District Attorney
Victim-Witness Assistance Program 310-458-5443
Rape Treatment Center, Santa Monica Medical Center ..310-319-4000
Sojourn Services for Battered Women 310-399-9239

Sanitation and Garbage

Sanitation District of Los Angeles County 213-685-5217

Shipping

Federal Express 213-687-9767
Postal Information 213-586-1737, 800-894-3433
United Parcel Service (UPS) 800-222-8333

Sports

California Angels 714-634-2000
Los Angeles Clippers 213-748-0500
Los Angeles Dodgers 213-224-1471
Los Angeles Kings 310-419-3160
Los Angeles Lakers 310-419-3182
UCLA Bruins 310-825-2101
USC Trojans 213-740-4072

Taxis

Checker Cab 310-201-0307
Super Shuttle 310-381-1111
Yellow Cab 310-273-5528
Yellow Taxi 310-201-0004

Stacey Ravel Abarbanel is a native of the San Francisco Bay Area, and has lived in the Los Angeles area from 1986-1987, and from 1990 to the present. Formerly the Promotion Manager for *Architectural Digest*, Abarbanel is a freelance writer. Her articles have appeared in *Meetings California*, a newspaper for the tourism industry, and *Ad LA*, a magazine for the Los Angeles advertising community. She has also recently completed *Smart Business Travel* for First Books. Abarbanel and her husband reside in Santa Monica.

THE ORIGINAL, ALWAYS UPDATED, ABSOLUTELY INVALUABLE
GUIDES FOR PEOPLE <u>MOVING</u> TO A CITY!

Find out about neigborhoods, apartment hunting, money matters, deposits/leases, getting settled, helpful services, shopping for the home, places of worship, belonging, sports/recreation, volunteering, green space, transportation, temporary lodgings and useful telephone numbers!

	#/COPIES			TOTAL
Newcomer's Handbook™ for Atlanta	_____	x	$13.95	$_____
Newcomer's Handbook™ for Boston	_____	x	$13.95	$_____
Newcomer's Handbook™ for Chicago	_____	x	$12.95	$_____
Newcomer's Handbook™ for Los Angeles	_____	x	$13.95	$_____
Newcomer's Handbook™ for New York City	_____	x	$16.95	$_____
Newcomer's Handbook™ for Washington, DC	_____	x	$13.95	$_____

SUBTOTAL $_____

TAX (IL residents add 8.75% sales tax) $_____

POSTAGE & HANDLING ($4.00 first book, $.75 each add'l) $_____

TOTAL $_____

SHIP TO:

_____
Name

_____
Title

_____
Company

_____
Address

_____ _____ _____
City   State   Zip

_____
Phone Number

FIRST BOOKS

Send this order form and a check or money order
payable to: First Books, Inc.

First Books, Inc., Mail Order Department
P.O. Box 578147, Chicago, IL 60657
312-276-5911

Allow 2-3 weeks for delivery.

Smart Business Travel

HOW TO STAY SAFE WHEN YOU'RE ON THE ROAD

Most of us take precautions every day to make our lives more safe. Business travel, however, presents a new and constantly changing set of circumstances that we don't deal with on a daily basis. This book offers simple tips that can make your business travel more secure. *Smart Business Travel* contains common sense as well as lesser-known but useful ideas that help the business traveler travel safely.

Don't be scared, be prepared!

	#/COPIES		TOTAL
Smart Business Travel	_____	× $12.95	$_____
TAX (IL residents add 8.75% sales tax)			$_____
POSTAGE & HANDLING ($3.00 first book, $.75 each add'l)			$_____
		TOTAL	$_____

SHIP TO:

_____
Name

_____
Title

_____
Company

_____
Address

_____
City   State   Zip

_____
Phone Number

Send this order form and a check or money order
payable to First Books, Inc.

First Books, Inc. Mail Order Department
P.O. Box 578147, Chicago, IL 60657
(312) 276-5911

Allow 2-3 weeks for delivery.

DO YOU THINK YOU KNOW LOS ANGELES BETTER THAN WE DO? TELL US!

If you are the first to offer any new information about
Los Angeles that is subsequently used in the next
Newcomer's Handbook™ for Los Angeles,
we'll send you a free copy of our next edition!

SUGGESTIONS:

_____

_____

_____

_____

YOUR NAME:

_____

YOUR ADDRESS:

_____

_____

Help keep this guide current! If a listing has changed, let us know.

UPDATES:

_____

_____

_____

_____

Send to: First Books, Inc.
P.O. Box 578147, Chicago, IL 60657

NOTES